Gifts to Men

Theological Perspectives

on Apostles

and Bishops

2nd Edition

JONATHAN E. ALAVARDO, DMIN, THM

Seymour Press

Lanham, MD

Gifts to Men: Theological Perspectives on Apostles and Bishops

Johnathan E. Alvarado

Copyright © 2019 Seymour Press
Lanham, MD 20706
All rights reserved.

ISBN-10: 1-938373-18-9
ISBN-13: 978-1-938373-18-3

Library of Congress Control Number: 2019934088

Unless otherwise noted, Scripture is taken from the New King James Version Copyright 1979, 1980, 1982 Thomas Nelson. Used by permission All rights reserved.

Printed in the United States of American by KDP

Seymour Press

Lanham, MD

Table of Contents

Foreword: Bishop J. Delano Ellis i

Preface: Dr. LaFayette Scales iii

Introduction
The Author, the Ministry, the Driving Question 1

Chapter I
*A Biblical Exploration of the Ministry
   of the Apostle* 19

Chapter II
A Biblical Basis for the Bishopric 43

Chapter III
*Apostles To Bishops: Historical and Theological
   Developments* 61

Chapter IV
*Contemporary Apostles: An Appreciation
   and Critique* 83

Chapter V
*Concluding Thoughts: Responses to
   Common Questions and Critiques* 103

Bibliography 125

About the Author 133

FOREWORD

To go anywhere and proclaim, minister and serve in God's kingdom is notable. To be sent by a recognized authority, to act in a prescribed way and carry out a specific task is a matter of honor and trust.

An apostle is a servant sent by an authority. He is sent with delegated power to accomplish a specified task. In the Hellenistic world a servant sent into a field to plant, cultivate crops and bring back a harvest to the owner was a sent one. A ship's captain was sent to a foreign country to trade, exchange and return to a king with treasure was a delegated sent one. A military general sent to conquer a territory, subdue kingdoms and return with the spoils to an emperor was a sent one.

Jesus was sent from the Father into the earth to conquer territory, establish a kingdom and return to the Father. Before He returned to the Father, He authorized twelve apostles to continue the work. "As my Father has sent me, even so send I you." (Jn 20:21b). These delegated servants continued His work to their death and passed the work on to regional bishops, early church fathers and martyrs who continued to oversee, guide and protect the work of the church. Church history records the transition from apostles to bishops was natural, incremental and well documented as a leadership continuum in the Lord's church.

Bishop Johnathan Elliott Alvarado masterfully explores the functions, linguistics and transitions of the call of an apostle and the office of a Bishop from a historical and contemporary perspective. There is much to rethink, learn and observe from his scholarly approach.

Dr. LaFayette Scales, Apostle
Rhema Christian Center Columbus, Ohio

PREFACE

Bishop Johnathan Elliott Alvarado's research and scholarship in "Theological Perspectives on Apostles and Bishops," has opened new doors of understanding for every serious student of apostleship and the bishopric. This work provides in one volume a major theological affirmation for Christian leadership in the Church of Jesus Christ.

His book takes us through unfamiliar waters of thought and broadens our historical overview of Christ's intention when He founded the Church. The bishop has been careful to keep us from the muddy waters of self-promotion but has shown us legitimacy and the path to it.

This work should prove to be of continuing usefulness. Our appreciation for the richness of the church universal will be stirred regardless to our differing affiliations.

As Chairman of the Advisory Board of the Joint College of African-American Pentecostal Bishops, Bishop Alvarado gives life and legend to all that we represent in the preparation of new leadership for the twenty-first century church. This writing becomes the flagship text of our concordat in Christ.

J. Delano Ellis II, Metropolitan-Archbishop

The Joint College of African-American Pentecostal Bishops

INTRODUCTION

The Author, The Ministry, The Driving Question

The Author

Every constructive theological work or position paper derives from a theologian who hails from a theological location. Some works originate from multiple theological loci that inform the finished product. This work is no different. What you hold in your hands are the reflections of a Pentecostal theologian who paused momentarily to consider theological matters of church government and ecclesiology. It is by no means the final word on the matter, nor is it broad enough to be the definitive treatise on such a vast inquiry. Rather, what you are reading is the theological journey of a Pentecostal pastor and scholar who paused for a moment to reflect out loud on the theme of Apostles and Bishops.

My hope is that this book will expand the readers' paradigm for church government (particularly within the African American Pentecostal Church) and provide a necessary resource for considering the theological implications of such a governmental expression. That hope is rooted in my core belief that the church is moving toward the image of Christ. Though there be distortions and maybe even aberrations, my belief is that the church is still pressing toward the prize of the high calling of God in Christ Jesus. As we study diligently and remain present to God in worship, I believe that the church will become the righteousness of God revealed in the earth. It is this hope that drives my research and fuels this project.

I write this book with that expectation, catalyzed by the various theological communities that have formed me. As a pastor, a bishop in the Lord's church, an academic leader, and a teacher, I find that the whole of my life has been geared toward following the trajectory of the Spirit in the here and now, while simultaneously exploring some of the age-old questions that have been asked by the church. I have endeavored to be faithful to the call of God in my inquiry and practice. That faithfulness has been expressed in my life through multiple church plants, multiple theological degrees, and multiple research projects/ publications designed to honor God and draw souls into the saving light of Christ. You see, I have endeavored to contribute to the formation of Christian belief because I am convinced that the root of some of our dysfunction is in our distorted belief systems.

The Ministry

Belief is central to the Christian faith. It is our belief in the Lord Jesus Christ that enacts our salvation and marks us as children of God. Believing the word of God revolutionizes our lives and gives us the power to live righteously in the world. Belief is an active outworking of an internal conviction, which often defies rational or logical thought. It is the core conviction that motivates our actions, informs our responses, and stabilizes us in an unstable world. Where our intellect, training, acumen, and exposure become woefully inadequate in a given situation, our belief becomes a sufficient cause for action.

As a matter of fact, belief and biblical faith are akin to each other in ways that cannot be easily dismissed. The major tenet of biblical faith is its requirement that some corresponding action occur in order for the internal conviction to genuinely be called faith. The same can be said of belief. It is the catalyst for action, which provokes an otherwise 'rational' and/or 'sound' person to live out convictions, which cannot often be substantiated with facts, figures, or scientific empiricism. Genuine faith often constrains persons to step out on seemingly nothing and do something significant and extraordinary simply because they believe. Apostles and Bishops have been charged with the responsibility for shaping and cultivating Christian belief. This has been and is central to their ministry and function within the Body of Christ.

I draw my thesis for belief, biblical faith, tradition, theology, and history, which Apostles and Bishops have been charged to steward, from greater minds than my own. These important theological loci seem to have been important and axiomatic for others who have contemplated our belief systems especially in the context of urban, contemporary ministries like many of ours. Ray Bakke, in his text *A Theology As Big As the City,* states it this way, 'This principle seems clear: the further one goes into the avant-garde frontier of creative ministry, the more important it becomes that we be deeply rooted in the biblical, theological and historical tradition. We need deep roots to survive in urban ministry.[1]

Many persons called Apostles and Bishops are so called because we had an internal witness and a community confirmation that prompted us to begin to reorient our lives around a persistent burden called 'service to the Lord.' Even though our circumstances or lives may not have appeared adequate or commensurate with that call, yet we believed! Even before we sensed the call to service, we were convicted at a more basic level concerning our own spiritual estate. We were somehow convinced that we salvation and that the cross of Calvary could rescue our lives if we simply believed.

My concern for the contemporary church and society more broadly, is going to be addressed in the various topics covered within this book. That concern is couched in the crisis of belief that I see prevalent in the church of the Lord Jesus

---

[1] Ray Bakke, A Theology As Big As the City, (Downers Grove, IL: Intervarsity Press, 1997), p.211

Christ. That crisis is injurious and detrimental to the survival of the church. It is principally a crisis of belief in the sense that we, who are called believers, have allowed our belief systems and articles of belief to be influenced and even altered by cultural or worldly systems. We who are called leaders (Apostles and Bishops) have in growing numbers ceased to believe as Christians and have begun believing as the world and, in some ways, we have begun to believe *in* the world.

Marva Dawn, in her book, *Reaching Out without Dumbing Down,* addresses this crisis of belief and depicts it as being rooted in a syncretism that has usurped the countercultural nature of the church in favor of a culturally accommodating belief system.[2] She asserts that it makes a serious statement that we do not seem to see as sufficient the tenets of the church of Jesus Christ, her history and tradition. In her estimation, this is evident in that we grasp for external affirmation from the world to validate us as the church. In other words, cultural accommodation and acceptance from the masses of the unregenerate for some churches and leaders trumps counter-culturalism and theological orthodoxy that should mark us as the people of God.

To a large degree, we have become recalcitrant in our responsibilities as apostles, bishops, and pastoral theologians, therefore our scholarship has gone lacking and our theological reflection has been shallow or non-existent.

---

[2] Marva J. Dawn, *Reaching Out without Dumbing Down: A Theology of Worship for This Urgent Time*. (Grand Rapids, MI: William B. Eerdmans Publishing Company, 1995), p. 297-303.

Many churches and leaders are now looking for the 'best tool' with which to grow the <u>church numeric</u>ally notwithstanding the injury that the church is suffering from this functionally utilitarian approach to ministry. It is our responsibility as Apostles and Bishops to infuse the life of the Holy Spirit into the life of the church such that our belief system is vibrant, living, culturally informing, and spiritually engaging. It is also our responsibility to have a belief system that is planted firmly within the text of Scripture and congruent with the faith that was once delivered. When we do this both spiritual and numerical growth will occur.

In my humble opinion there seems to be a drifting away from the transformative reality that an authentic relationship with Christ and His church will produce. The church in general has moved from a biblical or even orthodox belief system and settled for a way of being in the world that emphasizes functionality over substance. The prevalent mindset seems to be "if it works then it must be God." But we have failed to measure the criteria of what 'works' against the requisites of Scripture and tradition and therefore we are producing something that 'has a form of godliness... The definition of what 'works' should be drawn from the pages of sacred Scripture as modeled by our ecclesiastical progenitors. The Bible is our book for faith and practice and our ecclesiastical parents should be our examples, not the world and its appetites.

Orthodoxy, when understood as 'right belief,' is a word that has taken a proverbial beating throughout the history of the church. It has been associated with the bishops as stewards of the traditions of the church and thus bishops have also come under scrutiny and assault. This one important word has been cast in the light of dead, dry, lifeless ritual, devoid of the Spirit. It has been accused of being arrogant, dogmatic, restrictive, and narrow. Orthodoxy has found itself in the crosshairs of negative church growth campaigns like, 'the Church Sucks Challenge' and defamed by 'evangelistic' slogans like, 'Church for People who Love Jesus but Hate the Church.' It has asked Questions like, 'Do churchy people get on your nerves?' And, been polarized with talking points like, 'Church for People who don't do Church'! All of this has been done in the name of 'winning the lost.'

While I agree that dead rituals without a relationship with the Jiving Lord can drain the life out of a people and kill a church. It is equally true that vibrant, enthusiastic, spirited ritual devoid of an integrious belief system or a concrete theological substratum will decimate a people and eviscerate the theological vitality of any community. Proponents of leaderless churches and culturally based theological propositions are often more destructive than dead orthodoxy for they mislead adherents away from the claims of Christ and jeopardize their salvation. While those who enjoy such diminution of a faithful practice of orthodoxy in word and deed may rant and gloat, the fruit of their boasting has ripened. Many are eating it, but it is not satisfying.

It is because of this crisis of belief that I have written this book, in order to examine the duties and responsibilities of Apostles and Bishops who are charged to guide the churches' belief. In this endeavor, the creeds of the church can be helpful and provide much insight into how men and women of old have believed and what the basis of that belief was. As the church studies together, it is my hope and expectation that we will gain insight as to how the tenets of belief of our Christian patronage will inform our present belief systems. To the end that we will exit this reading with a deeper and more clearly defined understanding of what we believe and how that belief has been catalyzed by the Apostles and defended by the Bishops.

One of the earliest creeds of the church emerged in the second century and was a watershed for the basic beliefs of the church. It began as the Old Roman Creed because it originated with Christians in Rome but its later derivations came to be known as the Apostle's Creed. Though it did not attempt to address all of the matters of faith and doctrine in a single statement, it did speak to some of the major theological issues that had arisen during that time. It was an attempt by the early church leaders to clarify and codify where the church stood on such matters of belief. Though it is called 'the Apostle's Creed' the Apostles did not create it. Rather, it was created by second century bishops and used as the baptismal catechesis for initiation into the Christian community. It was so called because it reflected their synthesis of apostolic teaching.

Now this is interesting and telling concerning the nature of the church at that time. The canon of Scripture had not yet been crystallized so the leaders of the church did not have the benefit of a Bible, as we know it, as their rubric and guide. There were various heresies that were cropping up from without and within the church and the bishops felt it necessary to state definitively what the church believed.[3] This was not just a suggested statement, but rather for our early church fathers and bishops, to believe otherwise was to not be Christian. Especially in the face of such widely spread, popular, appealing, competing realities.

The reason that this book is important, is that the contemporary church is facing similar times and circumstances. Once again, the Apostles' doctrine and the Bishops' stewardship is required for the churches' survival. The church of the Lord Jesus Christ is now like at no other time in human history under the assault of competing realities and vying for the souls of men and women. There is so much wide spread ignorance and convoluted theological proliferation that a faithful witness has to be raised up in this time to herald the truth. The people of God are being bombarded with information of every sort on theological issues from the media and somewhere in the midst of it all the church must challenge the lies and raise the standard for authentic relationship with Jesus Christ.

---

[3] Roger Olson. The Story of Christian Theology. (Downers Grove, Illinois: InterVarsity Press, 1999), p. 28-31.

It is to this end that this text grapples with this very important topic on Apostles and Bishops and struggles with the ramifications and implications of their role in maintaining and promoting Christian belief. As we begin, we must examine documents like the historic Apostle's creed, understand its articles, and discern the circumstances surrounding its compilation. The greater the insight that we have, the more grounded we will be in what we believe. This requisite is upon us as Bishops and heralds of apostolic faith to reengage in the process of discovering and promoting a faithful Christian witness for the times in which we live. As God is our helper, we must face the ecclesiastical challenges of this day with solutions that promote the health and longevity of the Church of the Lord Jesus Christ.

The Apostle's Creed

I believe in God the Father Almighty, maker of heaven and earth; and in Jesus Christ his only Son our Lord; who was conceived by the Holy Ghost, born of the Virgin Mary, suffered under Pontius Pilate, was crucified, dead, and buried; the third day he rose again from the dead, he ascended into heaven, and sitteth at the right hand of God the Father Almighty; from thence he shall come to judge the quick and the dead. I believe in the Holy Ghost; the holy catholic church; the communion of saints; the forgiveness of sins; the resurrection of the body; and the life everlasting. Amen

The Driving Question

It has been my observation over the past several decades that a growing phenomenon has surfaced with respect to the church and its relationship to the world. It occurs to me that there has been a driving force from within the ranks of church leaders to manufacture a facade and foster a general disposition of the church that in my estimation is becoming more volatile and destructive. I do not speak of the necessary contextualization for the purposes of reaching and impacting the larger society with the gospel. Nor am I referring to some manifestation of the in breaking of the Kingdom of God in some radical or 'cutting-edge' ways. What I am directly addressing is the secularization of the values of the church beginning with the expressed value systems of some of the leaders of the church, many of whom having positions of great media notoriety and influence over the constituent Christian community.[4]

While this is mostly an American Church phenomenon, the insidious, carcinogenic effects are being felt all over the world. There seems to be a burgeoning and growing syncretism between the world's values and those of the church. Admittedly, I speak from the perspective of a churchman who has been thoroughly acculturated within the context of the African-American Church and whose ecclesiastical bent is derived from a Pentecostal, historical,

---

[4] *Johnathan E. Alvarado,* 'Twenty-First Century Holiness: Living at the Intersection of Wesleyan Theology & Contemporary Pentecostal Values' in Lee Roy Martin, ed., A *Future for Holiness: Pentecostal Explorations* (Cleveland, TN: CPT Press, 2013) pp. 237-240.

and orthodox position. I do however believe that the marriage of my personal history and my experience of living surrounded by this generational ethos gives me an opportunity to form holistic opinions and circumspect theological positions.

Ministering in this postmodern age is a daunting task to say the least. There are many axioms of societal life, which make it difficult to be effective in ministry today. The rapid change that society is constantly undergoing is a major factor in the way the church both sees and does ministry. Information of every sort on every topic both religious and secular is readily available. As Christians gain access to this information and ingest it, the problem of worldly syncretism is exacerbated because most do not have the filters or training mechanisms to sift through the voluminous potpourri of ideologies, philosophies, heresies, and pseudo-spiritual claims. The blessing of the 21st century information age has the potential to become the curse of orthodoxy in the church. This is why it is important to fortify the ministry of Apostles and Bishops who are charged to guide the church in the truth.

Moral relativism and situational ethics also have a prominent role in affecting the postmodern mind set. The absence of absolutes makes it difficult to establish the common ground of truth upon which a theological or moral line of reasoning can be based. This contributes to the moral free fall into which our society (and even the church) seems to be plummeting headlong. Within the contemporary church there seems to be more of an emphasis upon prosperous living than having a prosperous soul. Some leaders seem to be more interested in preaching the message of Christ without employing the methods of Christ in their lives and ministries. In other words, it is apparent to me that some wish to say what Jesus said but not live how Jesus lived, in modesty, humility, and servitude.

While these observations may be true in whole or in part, I am still optimistic for the future of the church. I still believe in this agency of God in the earth. Though some have seemed to hijack the church for their own purposes I still believe that God, through godly leaders, is redeeming the world unto Himself and unto His bride, which is the church. It is with this sense of optimism that I offer this study on the nature and character of Apostles and Bishops who form a great part of the leadership tier of the Christian community. It is my hope that this book will give the church a greater insight as to how to live faithfully unto God in the world.

It is my expectation that those who would lead in the church today would do so with a determination to recast the mold as to what living Godly in the world might look like. I am also fervently praying for God to raise up a generation of church leadership who do not set their personal or ministerial values based upon the world's standards of what is important, impressive, impacting, or spiritual. In the history of the church, there have always been those who strove for piety, humility, godliness, and modesty in the face of competing propositions for fame, grandeur, riches, and conspicuous indulgence. In our generation, now is the time for that decision to be made. I trust that as we make the right decisions both personally and professionally, that the church will reflect the biblical and orthodox community that God is desirous of cultivating in order to changing the world.

There are many ways in which the church has been described throughout history. Many terms have been used to give explanation and or analogy to help understand this agency of heaven in the earth. New Testament terms such as *ekklesia* (crowd, mob, or assembly of called out ones) or *kuriakos* (a group which belongs to the Lord) have been ascribed to the church in an attempt to give some sense of understanding of how the church functions and is most appropriately characterized. The Apostles and Bishops were instrumental in carving out the identity of the early church through their doctrine, lifestyle, and ministries.

The Old Testament uses terminology, which indicates that Israel was the people of God. Paul then borrowed that language and ascribed that terminology to the church (II Corinthians 6: 16). Peter also picked up on that language and characterized the church as the people of God (II Peter 2:9-10). Robert L. Saucy says that, 'the church is God's assembly; its beginning, its history and its glorious destiny all rest upon the initiative and power of divine grace. It is a people called forth by God, incorporated into Christ, and indwelt by the Spirit'[5] .Dr. Steven J. Land correctly asserts, 'the church as eschatological Trinitarian fellowship is a communion in God,

---

[5] *Robert L. Saucy, The Church in God's Program, (Chicago, IL; Moody Press,* 1972), 19.

a people of God, a body of Christ and thus a communion in the Holy Spirit.[6]

While these technical and theological definitions of the church may stretch our spiritual and intellectual sensibilities, they are not too difficult to grasp. For the purpose of our study, I would like to quickly give you several aspects of the covenantal Christian community (the church) that I have found beneficial to my understanding. As I list and expound upon these, I want each of us to think about what it means to be a part of a community such as this. As leaders, Apostles, and Bishops, I also want us to postulate as one who is not a part of the fellowship of any church. I want us to imagine what those on the outside see when they look at the modern church. In your opinion, does the image that the church in general gives to the world line up with God's intent for His church? How have we contributed to the world's negative estimation of the church today?

Understanding the nature of the church is extremely important today since so much individualism permeates our culture and societal ethos. It seems apparent to many people that church leaders are only interested in themselves and in their personal success. This is evidenced by the media portrayal of a few churchmen and women who seem to desire fame, fortune, and worldly standards of success. The ethos of the church as prescribed in sacred Scripture and throughout

---

[6] Steven J. Land, "The Triune Center: Wesleyans and Pentecostals Together in Mission", *(Pneuma: The Journal of the Society for Pentecostal Studies*, Volume 21, Number, 2, Fall 1999), 208-209.

early church history is just the opposite of that. From a biblical and historical perspective, the apostles and bishops should help the church be primarily concerned with the collective and the whole not the aggrandizement of the leader or the individual.

The church should be a reflection of God's intent for community and family in the earth. The challenge is that we have 'grown' churches today by selling them a bill of goods on personal and individual success that is contrary to the claims of Scripture and the intent of God. We have created a 'super-star' minister mentality, which postures the leader, as an icon or a celebrity. While honoring Christ's anointed leaders is important, many persons have unhealthily elevated some Christian leaders to 'star status' and made them the standard for ministry 'excellence.' In so doing, we have become, in this, imitators of the world and not of God. This is why living in community and abiding as a part of the church is of paramount importance, and this is why the ministry of the apostle and the office of the bishop are necessary, especially for today.

This is why I believe that there is no authentic Christian life apart from the church. To truly be Christian and to live faithfully unto God means to live as He has designed. The Scriptures bear record that the people of God were saved, lived, and worshipped together in community under the leadership of first the apostles and after that, the bishops. This truism flies in the face of modem, Americanized, teachings about rugged individualism, but it is rightly expressed in sacred Scripture, church history, and orthodox theology. Keith Drury said it like this, 'While it is possible to be a Christian without a pulpit, pews, or a pastor, it is unlikely that Christians will ever be Christians without *meeting* together. The assembly of believers has always been a central part of Christianity. Early Christians were willing to meet, despite the authorities and regardless of threats, punishment, and even execution. Christians have to meet together—it is what Christians do.[7]

The Bible gives record of how the ancient church operated and fleshed out its Christian life in the world in which they lived. The early church behaved in such a way that made an impact and left an indelible impression upon the larger society of the day. The biblical witness and the historical record reflect the leadership structure of apostles and bishops that fortified the church and framed its organization and Christian witness. We can now look back and see what it might have been like living in that time and belonging to that community. This book has been written to provide a window into the history and biblical substratum of the ministry of the apostle and the office of the bishop. As we examine how the pilgrim church lived and received apostles and bishops, we can draw out principles and apply them to our lives so that we might be an authentic people of God, and effective leaders for the advancement of the church on our watch.

---

[7]*Keith Drury, The Wonder a/Worship,* (Indianapolis, IN: Wesleyan Publishing House, 2005) p. 163.

CHAPTER ONE

A Biblical Exploration of the Ministry of the Apostle

Introduction

The ministry of the apostle is one of the foundational ministries of the Church of the Lord Jesus Christ. From the beginning, the church has been built upon the foundation of the apostles and prophets, Jesus Christ himself being the chief cornerstone. Paul lists the gift of the apostle as one of the ascension gifts that Christ left in the church 'for the perfecting of the saints for the work of the ministry.' Apostles were also missionaries who carried the message of Christ to the world.[1] Biblical scholars have looked at the gift and ministry of the apostle throughout church history and have discovered the multiform significance of the apostolate to the church.

---

[1] Herbert Lockyer, *All the Apostles of the Bible* (Grand Rapids, MI: Zondervan Publishing House, 1972) p. 7.

The original twelve apostles or 'Foundational Apostles'[2] were eyewitnesses of the ministry of Jesus Christ.[3] His selection of the twelve was a pivotal action in the establishment of the church. Other apostles were those who were closely related to the twelve, who heard the message and teachings of Christ.[4] One of the distinguishing features of the apostles was their proximity to Jesus. Their closeness to Him not only provided them with perspective but also with insight and opportunity to serve or practice ministry that would not have been afforded to them from a distance. Servants of Christ in the first century walked together with Jesus in concentric circles of intimacy observing, learning, and remembering what Jesus began to do and to teach.

There are generally three usages of the term 'apostle' in sacred Scripture. The three distinct usages of the term do not denote rank or order of importance. They simply delineate function. The first usage of this term refers to the twelve whom Jesus chose as foundational apostles or apostles of the Lamb. The second usage is with reference to disciples or leaders within the church being used as messengers of the church. The third usage is for special messengers (like Paul) being sent on special assignments from God.[5]

---

[2] The Apostolic Commission, *Apostolic Biblical Statement and Practical Guidelines* (IPHC, Apostolic Commission, 2007), p. 3.
[3] Giancarlo Biguzzi, "Witnessing Two by Two in the Acts of the Apostles" in *Biblica,* January 1, 2011, pp 2-3.
[4] Roger J. Olson, *The Story of Christianity Theology*, Downers Grove, IL: InterVarsity Press, 199, p. 25.
[5] 'Steve Bond, "Apostle" in Chad Brand, Charles Draper, and Archie England (eds.) *The Holman Illustrated Bible Dictionary* (Nashville, TN: Holman Bible Publishers, 2603) p. 88.

The idea herein and the overarching idea of the apostolate in general is official delegatedness.[6] All Apostles function within the scope of the authority of the one who sent them (in the case of the Foundational Apostles) or the communities that sent them (in most other cases).[7] , There are others who subscribe to a slightly different tiered delineation for apostles, but that dialogue will be taken up in chapter four.

Building upon the works of John J, Burkhard, Francis A. Sullivan, Herbert Lockyer, et al, this chapter will explore the ministry of the apostle, its biblical criterion, and its identifying markers. It seeks to give an overview of the work of recognized apostles in the text of Scripture and to make application of their work to the work of apostles today. It is my hope that upon completion of this chapter, readers will be able to recognize the gift of the apostle in the metanarrative of God's redemptive story.

Further, I desire that they be able to see their parallel narratives in light of the calling, gifting, and ministry of the apostle as understood in sacred Scripture. Because the scope of this chapter does not allow for a fully nuanced exposition of the ministry of the apostle, it should be read as an introduction and overview.

Working Definitions

The word apostle in the language of the New Testament is *apostolos.* This word means messenger or sent one.[8] The term 'apostle' was not originally germane to

---

[6] Robert Duncan Carver, 'Apostles and the Apostolate in the New Testament' in *Bibliotheca Sacra*, April-June 1977, p. 133.

[7] Ibid. p. 134.

[8] 'Bruce L. Shelley, *Church History in Plain Language* (Dallas,

spiritual or ecclesial matters. In the first century, this term spoke of a messenger in general, a herald, military persons, a fleet of ships, a passport, or a delegate. As Robert Duncan Carver postulates,[9] 'In Greek culture, religious messengers were called by other names, some of which are used in the Greek New Testament and are translated by such words as angel, messenger, preacher, etc....[10] Once the term 'apostle' began to be used to describe the disciples of Jesus who were carrying out His work, the term became 'sanctified' for that specific usage.

The apostles of our Lord Jesus Christ were dispatched with a particular message. They were commissioned to preach the saving knowledge of Christ and to recapitulate their memory of His exploits. Referencing the content of the apostles' message, Bruce Shelly posits,

> From the beginning, then, the apostles preached the resurrection of Jesus as the fulfillment of God's purpose announced in the Old Testament. The Messiah, once crucified, was exalted above the universe. Apart from that miracle, said the apostles, there is no gospel, no salvation, and no church.[11]

Within the broader Christian tradition, the term apostle has theological and ecclesiastical import that is generally understood to be with reference to Christ's servants of the first

---

TX: Word Publishing, 1995) p. 8.

[9] A. F. Walls, "Apostle" in L. Howard Marshall, A. R. Millard, J. I. Packer, and D. J. Wiseman (eds.) *New Bible Dictionary* (Downers Grove, IL: IVP Academic, 1996) p. 58.

[10] Robert Duncan Carver, 'Apostles and the Apostolate in the New Testament' pp. 131-132.

[11] Shelley. Church History, p. 15.

century who were charged to deliver His word, preserve His memory, and proclaim His deeds.

The term, 'the twelve' was a common reference in the gospels to the original disciples of our Lord, the foundational apostles who heralded his message to the world. Each of the four gospels bears witness to the fact that Jesus collected twelve disciples to train for the work of the ministry.[12] They were hand selected and commissioned to function as Christ's servants, friends, brothers, and successors. Their charge while with Jesus was to prepare for leadership roles after Jesus was gone.[13]

Twelve is a significant number that tethered the ministry of Jesus with the Jewish religious movement through which he and most of the initial Christians came. That number is so significant that even after Judas had deserted the company of the apostles, Paul still referred to them (1 Cor 15:5) as 'the twelve' even though at that point they were only eleven. This seems to indicate that, by that time, the term and its significance had begun to crystalize in the great tradition of the church.[14]

Twelve is an ecclesiastically significant number in that it has symbolic relatedness to the tribes of Israel and their relation to God[15] This further illumines the fact that the church grew out of or emerged from the theology, government, and history of Israel. The very number of the apostles chosen connected Jesus' movement with the

---

[12] Francis A. Sullivan, From Apostles to Bishops; The Development of the Episcopacy in the Early Church (New York: The Newman Press, 2001) p. 17.
[13] Ibid., 20.
[14] Ibid., 21.
[15] Ibid., p. 24.

patriarchal tradition of Israel. Thus, they maintained this tradition of 'twelve' with the appointment of Matthias until the foundational period of the church had passed.

The twelve have eschatological significance demonstrated through their realization and continuance of Christ's earthly ministry. John Burkhard posits, 'The Twelve, then, are the symbol of the covenant now entering into its final, eschatological realization by God's gracious will.'[16] The apostles of Christ carried on His earthly ministry with signs, wonders, healings, preaching, and teaching. As a matter of fact, part of the criterion for being named among the apostles according to Paul was to have had divine encounters, 'seeing the Lord' and/or miracles take place in one's ministry (1 Cor 9:1-2).[17]

Additionally, apostles should have church planting fruit credited to their labor, which is another demonstration of spiritual influence and the miraculous. Another criterion for the apostolate was that those who would be numbered with the twelve would have a particular insight into Scripture and the teachings of Jesus. Even though Scripture called the apostles 'ignorant and unlearned men' (Acts 4:13), the apostles amazed their hearers with spiritual insight into the ways of God because they had 'been with Jesus.'

The twelve is not a term that refers to an office or juridical function.[18] Christ's original apostles did not hold offices nor was the term 'apostle' an office but rather a function. Theirs was a unique role representing Israel's tribes

---

[16] John J. Burkhard, Apostolicity Then and Now: An Ecumenical Church in a Postmodern World (Collegeville, MN: Liturgical Press, 2004) p. 3.

[17] Sullivan, From Apostles to Bishops, p. 27.

[18] Burkhard, Apostolicity Then and Now, p. 5.

following, surrounding, being taught by, and being saved through, the Messiah.'[19] The apostles of the Lamb were principally charged to preserve the apostolic memory of the words and heroism of Jesus and to proclaim such with authenticity and zeal as eyewitnesses. This is likely why Jesus pulled the twelve unto Himself privately. Some scholars believe that He did so to foster an environment of in-depth teaching, that He might instruct them more fully than the other disciples.[20] This was because of the teaching responsibility that they were going to be charged to carry out after Jesus' death and resurrection.

Other apostles mentioned in Acts and the epistles functioned differently than did 'the twelve.' They were traditionally understood to be 'apostles of the churches' as opposed to 'apostles of Jesus Christ,' the preferred term for the apostle Paul.[21] The ministry of the apostles of the churches seems to be pointing toward other leadership functions within and without the church. They were often sent out as envoys, emissaries, or representatives of the church to herald the message of Christ evangelistically.

Their role paralleled the itinerant prophets of Israel.[22] Even through the second century of Christendom, the Didache mentions apostles and uses terms that indicate their parallel status with traveling prophets of that day.[23] Likewise, Papias, an Apostolic Father and Bishop of Hierapolis, is quoted to have received his catechism in the faith from

---

[19] Ibid.,9.
[20] Sullivan, p. 20.
[21] Ibid., p. 26.
[22] Burkhard, Apostolicity Then and Now 10-11.
[23] Didache, XI: in Henry Bettenson & Chris Maunder (eds.), Documents of the Christian Church (Oxford, England: Oxford University Press), pp. 70-71.

apostles who were taught by the apostle John.[24] This seems to illustrate the lenses through which the apostles of the church were seen in the first and second centuries.

Prudence demands that I make two other observations highlighting scriptural witness about apostles. First, it is clear, from the Greek language that Peter uses in Acts 1:20 while quoting from the Psalms, that his heart and intention for future church leaders was moving toward the bishopric. In Acts 1:20, Peter quotes David (Ps 69:25 and 109:8) with reference to Matthias, Judas' replacement and says, 'Let his dwelling place be desolate, and let no one live in it, his bishopric *(episcope)*, let another man take'. Peter's word choice is a clear indication that he is moving away from the language of 'apostles' to 'bishops.' He begins this transition in his own writings to the churches in Asia Minor as well (1 Pet 5:1). I will extend this concept further in Chapter Two where I exegete this passage from the Petrine corpus. I will however, comment more on Acts 1:20 in the next section of this chapter.

Secondly, it seems that another division of apostles existed that Paul addressed in the Corinthian communication. In Paul's defense of his apostolic authority (2 Cor 11:13-15) he discusses another category called 'False Apostles'. They were false apostles because their works did not match their claim. Sometimes referred to as 'super-apostles,' these men were boastful but did not know the Lord. They were engaged in the mixture of Gnosticism and Spiritual Judaism thus, in his insightful article, Doyle Kee comments,

---

[24] Fragments of Papias, 1.3-6, in ANF, 1: 153.

Our conclusion, then, is that the adversaries of Paul in Corinth were Hellenistic Jews who were propagating what we call "spiritual Gnosticism."

This, though, can be misunderstood because of a confusion as to exactly the identification of the "Christian Gnostics" of the early church.[25] Kee argues that early in the life and development of the church, false apostles arose who Kee argues that early in the life and development of the church, false apostles arose who had not settled basic theological convictions concerning the personhood of Christ, nor had they any fruit worthy of their apostolic claims. They only called themselves apostles, and in order to bolster their claim for legitimacy they compared themselves to a real apostle, Paul. Let us now look more deeply into a few scriptural accounts of the selection, divisions, and work of apostles.

Exegesis of Selected Passages

The gospel of Mark is divided into two halves with two sections each. Mark 3: 15 through 6:6, is the second section of the first half of the gospel of Mark.[26] One of the major themes of Mark's gospel is his interest in the twelve disciples and subsequently discipleship in general.[27] Mark 3: 13-15 chronicles Jesus' calling the twelve onto a mountain (similar to the covenant making mountain experiences of the Old

---

[25] Doyle Kee, "Who Were the 'Super-Apostles' of 2 Corinthians 10-13" in Restoration Quarterly, January 1, 1980, p. 69.

[26] Robert A. Guelich, Mark, World Bible Commentary (Dallas, TX: Word Books, 1989) p. 152.

[27] Larry W. Hurtado, Mark New International Bible Commentary (Peabody, MA: Hendrickson Publishers, 1989) p. 57.

Testament patriarchs) and ordaining or appointing the disciples to 'be with Him' . R. Alan Cole asserts that in so doing, Jesus begins the process of establishing His church with a break from the church of Israel.[28] Therefore, similar to the manner of Plato and Confucius, Jesus disciples were ordained that they might be in close proximity to the master.[29] They would be there to glean from His teaching and to learn His manner of life.

The secondary reason for their presence with Him was that they might be dispatched to do His bidding. 'Being with Jesus qualified the Twelve to bear witness to him and to participate in his distinctive ministry of proclamation and the overthrow of demonic power'[30] Their obedience to His call and response to His summons demonstrated their willingness to be available for the Master's use.

The theme of 'call' features prominently into Jesus' selection the twelve.[31] The call narratives of the apostles in this passage suggest that Jesus chose the ones He wanted in spite of their weaknesses and shortcomings.[32] These narratives also indicate the peculiarity or uniqueness of the call of the twelve. Their calling was one that had not been before, and would not be issued (in the same way) again in the future.[33] They were called to share in the power of the Kingdom of God and commissioned with a similar

---

[28] R. Alan Cole, Mark, The New Testament Commentary (Grand Rapids, MI: InterVarsity Press, 1989) p. 135.

[29] Ibid. p. 136.

[30] William L. Lane, Mark, New International Commentary on the New Testament (Grand Rapids, MI: William B. Eerdman's Publishing Company, 1974) p. 133.

[31] Guelich, Mark, p. 157.

[32] Hurtado, Mark, p. 58.

[33] Ibid., p. 62.

commission to Christ Himself, preach the gospel, cast out demons![34] In that way, the ministry of the twelve foundational apostles was to extend the ministry of Jesus throughout the region and throughout the first century.

The idea of ordination or appointment also takes on a special tenor in this passage. The complexity of the Greek syntax in verse fourteen makes the meaning somewhat difficult to ascertain, however the meaning of ordination or appointment in this text connotes a creative act as well.[35] This has tremendous implications for the selection of the twelve and the apostolate in general. Mark's use of the term 'made' or 'appointed' *(epoiaysen)* implies a divine act of creation wherein the disciples became something that they were not, prior to coming up the mountain with Jesus. Thus, they were the beginnings of the new creation of people in Christ, the church.[36]

Naming the twelve 'apostles' seems to be a secondary act.[37] Their function as preachers and exorcists was parenthetically included in Mark's record, highlighting the pivotal event of their mountain experience with Jesus, the act of their ordination or making. It seems that the first order of business for Jesus in this passage was to create a new and germinal people who would do Christ's bidding, not to name apostles. The 'newness' associated with their being 'made' or 'created' on the mountain derives from the root of the Greek word that Mark uses, (poiemai)'[38] This word is the basis of the

---

[34] Lane, Mark, pp. 32-33
[35] Guelich, Mark, p. 157.
[36] Ibid., pp. 158.
[37] Ibid., p. 158-159.
[38] Jerry Vines, Exploring the Gospels: Mark (Neptune, NJ: Loizeaux Brothers, 1990) p. 55.

English word 'poem' and is translated 'workmanship' in Ephesians 2:10. My synopsis of this dimension of the call is simple. Christ gives the name 'apostle' that is a description of function, only to those who have been created anew in Him, which is a reordering of their person.

My last thought about this passage centers around its focused use of the term 'apostle.' The Markan narrative follows the pattern of creating anew, for the purpose of naming, to the end that the apostles might be sent. The tension in this text lies in being ordained to 'be with' Jesus and subsequently being 'sent out' (apostelay) to preach and cast out demons. Obviously, one cannot 'be with Jesus' and 'be sent out' by Jesus simultaneously.[39] However, this text implies that one must reckon his or her apostolate to include missionary agency and exercise of the spread of the gospel if one is to truly be an 'apostle.' As recorded in this text, apostles do not languish in a parish or on friendly, comfortable shores, but rather they are active emissaries of the Kingdom, spreading the gospel, working miracles, and establishing the reign of God in the earth.

A careful exegesis of Acts 1:20-26 reveals much concerning the nature of apostolic ministry, the disposition of those who were apostles, and the expectations placed upon those who were in line to join the ranks of the eleven remaining foundational apostles. There is much theological significance in this narrative. Luke's account primarily emphasizes the continuity of the Christian story.[40] It is important to note that the Lukan idea of apostleship is not

---

[39] Guelich, Mark, p. 159.
[40] Peter Scaer, "Luke and the Foundations of the Church," in Concordia Theological Quarterly 76 (2012), p. 58.

confined to the book of Acts.[41] For a more robust understanding of Luke's vision of apostolicity, one must also consider Luke's gospel as well.[42]

The history of the twelve records that Judas defected from the ranks of the apostles and thus he lost his apostleship. His betrayal of Jesus was seen as the fulfillment of prophecy. Through his diabolical actions, he played a pivotal role in Jesus' death. His departure left a void within the ranks of the apostles; thus, the remaining apostles were burdened to select another apostle. The need to fill the vacancy was in part because of the apostles' propensity to see the church as an outgrowth of Judaism and a prophetic fulfillment of Israel.[43]

Luke's account of the elevation of Matthias in the book of Acts therefore, demonstrated their need for continuity between Israel and the church, and the prophetic continuity paralleled between the twelve apostles and the twelve tribes of Israel. According to Giancarlo Biguzzi, Matthias' addition to the ranks of the apostles restored the integrity to their numbers and brought them back into alignment.[44] To this point F. F. Bruce asserts, 'For those who believed that Jesus was the Messiah of David's line, this meant that many of the experiences of the psalmist (David) were understood as prophetically applicable to Jesus.'[45] Writing to God-fearers and gentiles, Luke demonstrated that the beginning of the

---

[41] F. F. Bruce, New International Commentary on the New Testament *Acts* (Grand Rapids, MI: William B. Eerdman's Publishing Company, 1988) p. 6.
[42] I Howard Marshall, TNTC Luke (Grand Rapids, MI: William B. Eerdman's Publishing. 1980) pp. 18-22.
[43] Scaer, "Luke and the Foundations of the Church," pp. 60-6.
[44] Biguzzi, 'Witnessing Two by Two in the Acts of the Apostles,' pp. 2-3.
[45] Bruce, Acts, p. 45.

church was not the end of Israel, but rather the fulfillment of it.[46]

According to the selection criteria outlined in Acts 1:21-22, the apostolate was reserved for the ones who had been with Jesus and the company of the disciples from the beginning.[47] The expectation the apostles placed upon one who was being considered for apostolic service, was that the person must have had some personal experience with the Master.[48] The one to replace Judas must be one who had travelled with Jesus and was familiar with his ministerial vision, goals, and accomplishments.[49] The replacement apostle must be one who had been faithful to Jesus' ministry from the beginning though he was not celebrated or featured.

The replacement apostle also had to be able to bear witness to the resurrection of the Lord Jesus Christ.[50] Jesus' resurrection was the watershed event in the life of the community of faith. The power of the apostolic witness rested upon the fact that they had seen Him resurrected.[51] Therefore, the confidence to give personal testimony and witness to the resurrection of the Lord was a necessary criterion in selecting the apostle to replace Judas. It is not clear in the text as to whether or not Judas' replacement would be chosen from the ranks of other apostles of Christ to become one of the twelve,

---

[46] Scaer, "Luke and the Foundations of the Church," pp. 59-60.

[47] Marshall, Luke, pp. 65-66.

[48] Bruce, Acts, p. 46.

[49] French L. Arrington, The Acts of the Apostles: Introduction, Translation, and Commentary (Cleveland, TN: Pathway Press, 1998) p. 15

[50] Ibid.

[51] David J. Williams, Acts, New International Bible Commentary (Peabody, MA: Hendrickson Publishers, 1990) p. 33.

or whether such a selection should come from the rank and file disciples who walked with Jesus.[52]

The replacement apostle was to take his place in the ministry and apostleship that Judas deserted to go to his own place. This is an important distinction as it pertains to the ministry goals and aspirations of the apostles. There seems to have been two ways that Judas (and all of the apostles) could have gone. He could have taken his place in the ministry and apostleship given to him by Jesus, or he could have taken 'his own place.' He chose the latter, and in so doing discovered the recompense for operating in self-will.[53] Peter's stem recapitulation of Judas' final estate is a warning to all who function in ministry seeking their own way.

Matthias received the apostolic appointment and was numbered with the eleven making them complete and fulfilling all righteousness. This action was significant in light of the previous discussion on the number twelve and the symbolism of 'the twelve.' Some have argued that Matthias' appointment was premature and that the company of apostles should have waited, holding a space for Paul.[54] That logic defies the unique nature of Paul's apostolate. The topic of Paul's apostolate will be discussed later in this chapter.

Eusebius reports Matthias to have been one of the seventy disciples reported in Luke 10:1 who was sent out two by two.[55] Ultimately, tradition reports that Matthias became a missionary to Ethiopia.[56] No matter the outcome of Matthias

---

[52] Marshall, Luke, p. 66.
[53] Ibid.
[54] Bruce, Acts, p. 48.
[55] Eusebius, HE 1.12.3.
[56] Bruce, Acts, p. 46.

apostolate, one cannot deny the theological significance of his appointment to the apostolate. Since Matthias was an apostle whom Christ Himself did not select, one must ask were there other apostles functioning within the Body of Christ during that time?

First Corinthians 15:3-7 seems to indicate that there were many apostles preaching, teaching, and ministering, during and shortly after Jesus lived. When one considers Paul's recollection of the post resurrection appearances of Christ, Paul's delineation of the persons to whom Christ showed Himself requires careful analysis. First, Cephas who we know as Peter saw Christ. This is reasonable in that Peter was a leader whom Christ chose, rehabilitated, and authorized to lead the twelve. Second, Christ appeared to 'the twelve.' Third, a company of five hundred brethren saw Him. Fourth, James the brother of Jesus saw Him, and finally, all the apostles. We may speculate as to the omission of the others to whom Christ appeared[57] (particularly the women at the tomb), but our discussion centers around two of the three groups of persons listed.

The curios notion is the obvious distinction made between 'the twelve' and 'all the apostles.' Given the exactitude with which that term, 'the twelve' has been used throughout the gospels and Acts, it is fair to assume that Paul and his contemporaries had a certain understanding of that term. Paul's familiarity with 'the twelve' would certainly cause him to mean the foundational apostles of the Lamb (and no one else) when using that term. Also, he would not have needed to mention 'all the apostles' if he were only speaking

---

[57] Leon Morris, 1 Corinthians, The New Testament Commentary (Grand Rapids, MI: William B. Eerdman's Publishing. 1985) p. 202.

of 'the twelve' and he would not have needed to mention 'the twelve' if he were lumping them in with 'all the apostles. The only logical conclusion to be drawn is that Paul was speaking of 'the twelve' and of 'all the apostles' as two distinct groups of apostles functioning within the Body of Christ.

Leon Morris contends that there is no real distinction between the two terms and that Paul's mention of 'all the apostles' who saw Him likely refers to Christ's ascension.[58] The problem with that interpretation is that there were clearly only 'the twelve' present at His ascension in Acts 1:1-3. Jesus showed himself to 'the twelve' on several post resurrection occasions. Why only point out the ascension when Paul mentions 'all the apostles'? Following that logic, 'all the apostles' could have referred to any of the appearances to 'the twelve' and thus there would not even be any need to specifically point out' all the apostles' as a separate group to whom Jesus appeared.

Marion Soards postulates that there is distinction between the two references.[59] He highlights the importance of 'the twelve' to the developing early church, noting that Paul affirms this notion. Also important to him was the visibility of the resurrection to all of the witnesses of Christ. Paul seems to relish the fact that the historical reliability of the resurrection was not in question in the face of so many witnesses. Finally, Soards sees 'all the apostles' as a distinct group of disciples. He postulates[60] that Paul may be referring to the fact that all of the witnesses saw the resurrected Lord

---

[58] Ibid., P. 203..
[59] Marion L. Soards, 1 Corinthians, New International Bible Commentary (Peabody, MA: Hendrickson Publishers, 1999) pp. 319 -320.
[60] Ibid., p. 320.

and that they all may have a secondary apostolic function as a result of that sighting. To that end Soards comments thusly, 'Those who saw the risen Lord were ultimately those who were "sent out ones" (apostles).[61]

Gordon Fee weighs in with clear and definitive insights for consideration. First, he affirms the uniqueness of 'the twelve' as the group who Jesus called up the mountain to be with Him.[62] He contends that the latter naming of 'all the apostles' clearly referenced another group of disciples who had seen the Lord.[62] Fee asserts that the persons within the group designated 'all the apostles' was not clear but he was resolute hat they were a different group from 'the twelve' with perhaps a different function.

He goes on to say, 'The Twelve were a definite group who had a special relationship to Jesus and in the early church probably served in some kind of authoritative capacity. But the "apostles," a term that included the Twelve, were a larger group who in Paul's understanding had seen the risen Lord and were commissioned by him to proclaim the gospel and found churches' .[63] This clear distinction indicates that there were greater numbers of apostles, not necessarily of the same function as 'the twelve,' but certainly of value and functionality to the Kingdom of God. Of 'the twelve,' Judas was the only foundational apostle that was replaced. The others, including those encompassed in the group 'all the apostles' carried on the functions of 'the twelve' to the degree that they could without the authority to function fully or

---

[61] Ibid.

[62] Gordon Fee, *The First Epistle to the Corinthians*, New International Biblical Commentary, (Peabody, MA: Hendrickson Publishers, Inc., 1984) p. 729.

[63] Ibid. pp. 729-30.

completely as 'the twelve' did. These were the ones for whom Paul gave testimony. Now our attention turns to apostles who lacked credibility and standing within the Christian community.

The scathing indictment of Revelation 2:2 indicates that there were false apostles present within the churches and itinerating between the churches in Asia Minor. Not too long into the second half of the first century, voices emerged claiming apostolic authority without apostolic credibility. They came to Ephesus, a chief city in Asia Minor, whose trade routes and uninitiated and mostly gentile converts made it easier (so they thought) to perpetrate a fraud and impose their will upon the churches for pecuniary gain.[64] These were self-willed men who traded in genuine faith for pretense and license. This made for difficult ministry conditions in the late first century.

The church in the city of Ephesus was the only church of the seven mentioned in Revelation to have its founding recorded in the Book of Acts.[65] Paul labored with them almost two years securing them in the faith.[66] Timothy spent time establishing then according to one of the epistles that bears his name (I Tim 3:1-5). History records that John, when released from Patmos spent his last years in the city ~~of Ephesus~~.

This church was one of good works, and those good works gave it credible witness in the city of Ephesus.[67] They

---

[64] Ibid. pp. 731 – 7Wall, p. 70.32
[65] Leon Morris, *Revelation*, The New Testament Commentary (Grand Rapids, MI: William B. Eerdman's Publishing Company, 1987) p. 58
[66] R. Hollis Gause, *Revelation: God's Stamp of Sovereignty on History* (Cleveland, TN: Pathway Press, 1998) p. 48.
[67] Morris, Revelation, p. 59.

had been established in the faith through trial and difficulty from without, but now outside voices were infiltrating the young church. They were bringing unlawful messages of division and Judaizing. Robert Mounce, in his thorough commentary asserts, 'The false apostles mentioned have been variously identified as Judaizers from Jerusalem (as in 2 Cor 11:13-23), Nicolaitans (v. 6), or any self-styled apostles who claimed a position over that of the local elders.[68] False apostles were exerting considerable amounts of pressure on the young church hoping to gain a foothold.

The problem of these false apostles was multifaceted. First, they were from without, proffering mixed messages of paganism and accommodation with the surrounding social and religious order.[69] Secondly, they came from without, not adhering to the doctrine and the 'faith once delivered to the saints.' Third, these men were not just deceived as to who they were; they were also deceivers of the church.[70]

These outside voices called themselves 'apostles.' However, they taught doctrine that put the church in bondage to the law, conjured special revelations in order to bring the church under their control, and disparaged the foundational and legitimate apostles who originally established the church at Ephesus.[71] Robert Mounce asserts, "The context suggests that the self-appointed apostles were antinomians rather than legalists' thus, they advocated for a brand of Christianity

---

[68] Robert W. Wall, *Revelation*, New International Bible Commentary (Peabody, MA: Hendrickson Publishers, 1991) p. 70.

[69] Gause, Revelation, p. 49

[70] Robert H. Mounce, *The Book of Revelation*, New International Commentary on the New Testament (Grand Rapids, MI: William B. Eerdman's Publishing Company, 1998) p. 68

[71] Walls, p. 70.

without stricture or regula fide."[72] This was challenging for the fledgling church, but they responded in a way that merited Jesus' commendation.

Ephesus' remedy for false apostles was to test their apostolic claims against the watermark of legitimacy.[73] They rejected the false claims of those who had no apostolic fruit to their credit. Hollis Gause comments on their actions thusly, "The Ephesians put these men on trial, and proved that they were liars (Rev 2:3). Such intolerance of evil is a spiritual virtue."[74] Their example of zeal for the legitimate should inspire the church to strive in all of our doing to be found in the will and purpose of God.

Final Thoughts on Apostolicity

My concluding thoughts on apostolicity are but a break in this discussion. I recognize that I have broached a broad and far reaching topic, and more conversation is necessary in order to adequately realize a theological position on the apostolate. There is much more that could be said about important and relevant themes rooted in this discussion such as, cessationism, apostolic authority, open and closed canon, and apostolic succession. Some of those important topics will be taken up in the latter chapters of this book. Others must be left for another discussion altogether. The purpose of this chapter has been to initiate that conversation and to give some possible starting points for future dialogue. As I bring this

---

[72] Morris, Revelation, p. 59
[73] Gause, Revelation. p. 49
[74] Mounce, *The Book of Revelation*, p. 69

portion of the book to a close, here are some potential theological loci for further exploration.

Paul, according to John Burkhard, was the apostle par excellence.[75] Burkhard affirms Paul's singular and unique status as the apostle sine qua non. Likewise, in his seminal work on church history, Bruce Shelley says, 'No man—other than Jesus, of course—has shaped Christianity more than Saul (or, as Christians came to say, Paul, a name more familiar to the ear of Greek-speaking people). No one did more for the faith, but no one seemed less likely.[76] Luke, in the book of Acts, goes through much effort to demonstrate to the Christian community that Paul was a foundational apostle with the status and authority equal to Peter, his counterpart to the Jews.[77] Servants and apostles alike would do well to follow in his footsteps and emulate his apostolate.

One must remember that preservation of Apostolic Memory was one of the primary functions of the foundational apostles. Apostolic memory was the body of common truth that the apostles shared and disseminated to the Christian community. As the church began to spread geographically, the apostles were charged with spreading the story of Christ and His heroism throughout the surrounding regions. Each apostle with his assigned mission field went about heralding the good news and protecting the narrative from corruption and error. It required that they have a dogged affinity for the true history of Christ and His church, and it required that they evaluate others who sought to gain

---

[75] Morris, Revelation, p. 59
[76] Gause, *Revelation*, p. 49
[77] Burkhard, 12.

access to the Christian community by their own adherence to the story.

Finally, it is important to note that the post-apostolic period saw a dramatic rise in intellectual pursuit and theological rigor.[78] In order to maintain the aforementioned apostolic memory, the successors to the apostles had to begin to rehearse and codify the historical theological development of the church for posterity. They were required to defend the faith, systematize the theology of the church, maintain the memory of Jesus, and prognosticate the direction of the Christian community within the larger society. They were responsible for defending the faith in an increasingly complex world. Thus, they gave themselves over to apologetic prowess and conscripted themselves to intellectual theological pursuits.

As the church continued to grow and expand, the leadership of the church began to morph and take on contextual forms as well. The foundational apostles began to die off and with the exception of Judas; none of them was replaced as a foundational apostle. The responsibility for leading the church into the future became the responsibility of another group of leaders within the church. The next chapter will examine their biblical moorings, historical development, and theological significance to the early church. It is my hope that the readers of this text will track with me as we follow the trajectory of the history and theology of the church toward an understanding of apostles and bishops.[79]

---

[78] Shelly, Church History, p. 19.
[79] Scaer, "Luke and the Foundations of the Church." p. 66.

CHAPTER TWO

A Biblical Basis for the Bishopric

Introduction

The office of the bishop is one of three offices expiated in the Pauline Corpus. It was instituted in the Apostolic Era and crystalized during the Patristic Period. Forging a biblical understanding of this ecclesial office is the first step toward solidifying a robust and nuanced theology of the office of the bishop for contemporary churches, fellowships, and denominations. Building upon the exegetical work of Donald Guthrie, Gordon Fee, Ayo Adewuya, William Mounce, Wayne Grudem, et al, this chapter will explore some biblical considerations for the office of the bishop. The theological implications of the texts will be cursorily examined in this chapter, but a robust and nuanced theology of the episcopacy will be reserved for future chapters.

This chapter seeks to provide the readers with an overview of the work of the bishop as prescribed and described in the text of Scripture. Herein, I will carefully exegete key passages of sacred Scripture, mining them for insights and detailed understanding of the work, office, and ministry of the bishop. This will be done with a view toward application of biblical principles to contemporary ecclesial contexts. Though there are several passages that allude to the work and ministry of bishops, I have selected three texts upon which I will build my argument.

These texts give insight into the role of the bishop and the function of ministerial leadership that he or she provides. These texts also outline biblical requirements for the office of a bishop in the Lord's church and of a shepherd of a local congregation. The biblical precedent for this expression of government is supported in sacred Scripture and can be seen developing throughout church history. It is my hope that this style of government as it is set forth in this treatise will be seen as scripturally viable, historically accurate, and an effective model of church leadership for the twenty-first century. As we revision the church in this Episcopal order and recapitulate some ancient themes of the pilgrim church, I will argue for the stability that this form of government produces. I make my claim in light of what I have observed in the varied and often times injurious leadership strategies and structures that exist in the church today.

I recognize that there are several legitimate models of government in and for the church today. However, I contend that many leadership fads, trends, and common practices are simply imitations of secular managerial style, rather than biblically based, theologically sound, culturally relevant models for church leadership. Functional utilitarian forms of government designed to attract the masses rather than disciple the redeemed have too often supplanted biblically grounded leadership. If my observation is near accurate, the tenor of the times requires serious leaders to employ historically viable and ecclesiastically legitimate forms of government if we are to honor God within the church and represent God to the world. As we explore the potential of the bishopric as a leadership office within the church, let us open our minds to what possibilities may exist to coalesce churches into the Body of Christ.

When one accepts the call and receives the appointment to the sacred and holy office of bishop, along with the rank that it affords and the dignities associated with the appointment, one must also embrace the biblical framework in which it was cast. The bishop must be willing to bear the burden of the office as outlined in sacred Scripture. He or she must seek to honor God in his or her deportment, conforming life to the precepts of holy writ and living sacrificially as unto the Lord. The bishop must soberly enter into the fraternity of self-diminishing imitators of our Lord Jesus Christ, who 'emptied himself' of divine prerogatives for the sake of humanity's salvation. Only then will the bishop be pleasing to God and a servant to the people.

The goals of this chapter are to explore the biblical foundation for the office of the bishop paying particular attention to the Pentecostal Charismatic dimensions of the early church. Secondly, this chapter has been written to describe the historical progression and development of the office of the bishop beginning with the Apostolic Era up to the Patristic Period. Finally, this chapter will frame the argument for episcopacy within the text of Scripture examining three texts as foundational for an understanding of the office of the Bishop.

Exploration and Exegesis of Key Passages

It seems to me that I Timothy 3:1-7 is the hallmark text for the office of the bishop. In it, Paul sets forth the criterion for Episcopacy and sets the bishop apart as one of only three 'offices' that he mentions in his correspondence to the church. Those three offices mentioned are Bishop (I Tim 3:1-7), Elder/Pastor (Tit 1:5-9), and Deacon (I Tim 3:8-13). The same three-tiered leadership structure is employed by Ignatius of Antioch in the next century and becomes the preferred structure for church government for 1500 years.[1] Having said that, I will visit this topic in chapter three. Suffice it to say, there were at least two main reasons that bishops were set into the church in the first century.

The first reason is found within the larger pericope of I Timothy where Paul was addressing some issues of community worship for which the presence and authority of the bishop would be needed. The presence[2] of the bishop was

---

[1] Justo L. Gonzalez, *The History of Christian Thought Volume I: From the Beginnings to the Council of Chalcedon.* Nashville: Abingdon Press, 1970, p. 77.

[2] Gordon Fee, *1 and 2 Timothy, Titus*, New International Biblical Commentary, (Peabody, MA: Hendrickson Publishers, Inc., 1984), pp. 78-79.

typically to keep order and maintain the vanguard concerning spiritual things in worship.[3] The second reason for bishops was to protect the church from false teaching.[4] The presence of false teachers in the early church was a clear and present danger. The rise and embrace of Gnosticism within the Christian community necessitated shepherds of local congregations who knew the truth of the gospel and could teach that truth to the faithful.[5] One of the main responsibilities of the bishop was to be the guardian of the tenets of the faith, the teachings of Christ and the Apostles so that those truths could continue to be taught in perpetuity. The office of the bishop was established to accomplish these two main purposes.

Worship, as a key aspect of the scope of responsibilities of the bishop, was given high priority in the life of the bishop. As Paul 'got down to business' in this passage, he addressed the importance and the scope of prayer for the church in Ephesus where Timothy provided leadership (I Tim 2:1-4). He gave Timothy the responsibility to lead the church in prayer (the term 'prayer' can be synonymous for worship) around themes that were germane to the common good. As a matter of fact, these prayers were focused more toward the government and the civic order

---

[3] Donald Guthrie, *Tyndale New Testament Commentaries: Pastoral Epistles*, (Grand Rapids, MI: William B. Eerdman's Nelson Publishing. 2000), pp. 79-81.

[4] William Mounce, *The World Biblical Commentary: Pastoral Epistles*, (Nashville, TN: Thomas Nelson Publishers, Inc. 2000), pp., 152-153.

[5] Justo L. Gonzalez, *The Story of Christianity: Volume 1 The Early Church to the Dawn of the Reformation.* (New York: Harper Collins Publishers, 1984) pp. 58-61.

than toward the saints. Paul charged Timothy to lead the church in praying on behalf of the world so that the church could experience a peaceful and tranquil life.

Could it be that the liturgical and celebrative work of the bishop should principally be within the church but with an outward focus to the good of the larger society around the church? Could one surmise that the work of the bishop is principally couched in liturgical celebration, ritual, and true worship? It seems that Paul's concern for kings, authorities, and civil order was for the good of those directly involved and affected by it, and also for the serenity of the church. Paul's directives seem to indicate that a bishop in the Lord's church should never forget that the scope of his or her mission has broader implications and further reaching ramifications than that which takes place within the walls of one's local judicatory and that worship reaches beyond those boundaries influencing the extremities.

Timothy was also interested in keeping the church from false teaching. You see the Greco-Roman world into which the church was birthed was alive with religious syncretism and pluralism. Many of the 'mystery religions'[6] being practiced in the Greco-Roman society into which the church was born had their origins in ancient fertility rites and cultic practices involving meals and they were influential in the lives of the citizens. These meals foreshadowed the Christian celebration of Eucharist and scholars still vary in opinion as to which celebration (pagan or Christian) was the

---

[6] Gonzalez, *A History of Christian Thought Volume I*, p. 54.

originating rite.[7] Finally, the influence of Rome on the early church cannot be underestimated,[8] Not all of Roman influence was injurious to the church, however some was. Therefore, Roman influence must be understood at the very least as a mitigating factor when seeking to understand Paul's admonition to Timothy to steward the doctrine of the church.

During this embryonic phase of the episcopacy the bishop was principally a local church officer. But as the church developed, the office of the bishop was expanded to include territories and regions.[9] This may be because of the necessity for the bishop to shepherd the doctrine being taught within the local churches and to see him or herself as having spiritual influence on governmental, civic, and social structures that surrounded the church. Therefore, through leading the church in worship, the bishop maintained a watchful eye on the doctrine being taught and provided spiritual covering and care for the city, region, or municipality in which he or she served.

In chapter three, Paul indicated to Timothy that desire is a key component for ascension to the office of the bishop. He asserted that those selected for this office must desire or set their heart to function in it with grace and dignity. This speaks to the desire one must have to serve as a bishop and it also indicates how important it is for the bishop to conform his or her desires to those things, which become a bishop. Paul

---

[7] Ibid., 55-58.
[8] Ibid., pp. 59-60.
[9] Mounce, pp. 153-155, See Guthrie, p. 91.

described the work of the bishop as (kalou) good work. Other translators prefer the term 'noble' to clarify the quality of the work of the bishop.[10] Nobility not only speaks to the quality of the work to be performed but also to the motive behind performing the work. In this passage, Paul argued that bishops must have pure motives coupled with excellent work.

Paul gives some indication of the gravity of the assignment of the bishop through the stringency of the criterion for acceptance into the bishopric. Though the actual criterion delineated in the text is important, my purpose in this chapter is not to argue the interpretive nuances of whether women can be bishops, or whether single men can be bishops. I am not as interested in whether being 'the husband of one wife' means one wife at a time thus indicating that a divorcee or widower can or cannot serve as a bishop. These are important and worthy discussions. However, the scope of this chapter does not allow for a full exegetical expiation of the text. What is clear in the text is that the selection of a bishop was taken seriously and criterion for becoming a bishop was arduous, considered over time, and heavily scrutinized.

I cannot help but notice the lack of mention of 'supernatural' criterion from Paul to Timothy. In this hallmark passage Paul seems to focus on lifestyle criterion (the maintenance of which is in and of itself supernatural) without any serious examination of what charismatic endowments the candidate for episcopacy may possess. It seems apparent to me that Paul was more interested in

---

[10] Guthrie, p 91.

bishops being stable, mature, moral leaders who could convince others through their witness and lifestyle. Rather than being the creators of doctrine or the workers of miracles (as the apostles and certainly the twelve were), in Paul's mind bishops needed to be learned guardians of the truth and of good reputation so as to have credibility when they told and retold the stories of the heroism of Christ and the apostles.

Similarly, in the book of Titus 1:5-7, Paul gave two directives to his disciple Titus. His emphasis upon these two things so early in the salutation of his letter could be an indication that the church in Crete, the city where Titus served, was not as organized as the church in Ephesus, the city where his counterpart Timothy was serving.[11] Paul's assertion of his apostolic identity and authority so forcefully and his truncated greeting to Titus in the first few verses of the chapter indicated an urgency to his request.[12] It seems to me that as a servant and spiritual son, Titus was assigned to the place where his spiritual father Paul deemed his skills and anointing were necessary. Also, it seems that even though the question of Paul's apostolic authority was not as pronounced in Crete as it was in Ephesus, it was still of concern to Paul, thus the protracted introduction.[13]

Apparently, Titus had the constitution, organizational skills, and grace upon his life to go into chaotic situations and bring order. Paul left Titus with the two-fold assignment to

---

[11] Guthrie, p. 196.
[12] Fee, 167-70.
[13] Mounce, pp. 377-378.

'set in order the things that are lacking and ordain elders (episkopos) in every city.' While this is a specific instruction to Titus, in my estimation, it contains universal applicability for all those who walk in the office of the bishop. This directive from Paul indicates that every bishop should take part in the organization of the church in his or her city. Thus, bishops must have city influence. Paul's rationale and assignment of Titus to Crete seems to indicate that every city needs at least one bishop to unify the church, organize the mission, and stabilize the people. Paul's mandate for setting in governmental leaders is one of the earliest recorded models of a crystallized church government and structure.

This passage demonstrates that Paul and Titus understood that the duties of the office of the bishop were at least in part to elect, assign, or appoint other bishops (elders) in cities, to set the church in order, and to multiply the church in the surrounding regions. This denotes that they saw church planting, development of leaders and local churches, and city influence as some of the primary characteristics of an authentic bishop. Also, organizing and insulating the church from error were two of the principle functions Titus was tasked to undertake.[14] Though this mandate was specifically given to Titus, I believe that it has universal applicability for every bishop. As we saw in Paul's admonition to Timothy, doctrinal fidelity was a premium. We see it again here in Titus and I believe we should look for it in the last passage we will examine.

---

[14] Ibid., 385.

My exegesis of I Peter 5:1-4 points out at least three things that are important to our study of the bishopric. Those three things are important because they help the reader see the progression of the church in nomenclature and functionality of leadership. First, the auto-ethnographic language that Peter uses connects his ministry function with his self-identification as both an apostle and a bishop in the Lord's church. Second, this passage affirms the collegial nature of church government and the mutual respect and submission that episcopates must have one for the other. Finally, this passage warns against the moral, spiritual, and doctrinal corruption that can and often does come to leaders within the Body of Christ. These three scriptural insights allow for an expanded view of biblical episcopacy and ground the thesis of this chapter with biblical moorings.

When Peter introduced himself to his readers in chapter one, verse one, he self-identified as an apostle. In Peter's case this connotes a special status and authority given by Christ Himself for Peter to speak on Christ's behalf.[15] Though the term apostle (*apostolos*) was used to describe messengers in a common or secular sense prior to the advent of Christ and His church, usage of the term subsequent to Christ's advent took on new meaning.[16] This is because Christ selected, empowered, and dispatched 'the twelve' to

---

[15] Norman Hillyer, *I and 2 Peter*, New International Bible Commentary, (Peabody, MA: Hendrickson Publishers, 1992), p. 25.
[16] Peter H. Davids, *The First Epistle to Peter, New International Commentary on the New Testament* (Grand Rapids, MI: William B. Eerdmans Publishing Company, 1990), p. 45-46.

accomplish His purposes with special grace and authority.[17] Peter recognized that he had been called for a special purpose and commissioned by Jesus to advance the church. He also recognized that others were called alongside him who in their writings often used the term 'apostle' as well.[18]

The interesting turn of title comes in chapter five. When Peter exhorts the leadership of the churches of the Asiatic diaspora, he greets them as elders *(presbuteroi)* and himself as a fellow elder *(sumpresbuteros)*, not an apostle. He seems to understand and imply what I assert in this chapter, that apostles can and do function as elders/bishops in the Lord's church. This turn of phrase may be an indicator that Peter recognized that his colleagues who were soon to be successors would need new ecclesial designations based upon what they were called to do. The hierarchical nomenclature that Peter employs, likely stems from the fact that the churches of the Jewish diaspora were structured in the fashion of the Sanhedrin Council, which had a well-organized hierarchy and a president of the council.[19] Like Paul whose Jewish heritage and orientation related to and presupposed ecclesial hierarchy, Peter's usage of the term 'elder' indicates an office rather than age or seniority among the people.[20] Though the early churches were not completely and finally structured, Peter likely saw himself functionally transitioning to another tier of ministry and recognized that

---

[17] Wayne Grudem, *I Peter*, The Tyndale New Testament Commentary, (Grand Rapids, MI: William B. Eerdmans Publishing Company, 1988), p. 47.
[18] Ibid., p. 21.
[19] Hillyer, I and 2 Peter, p. 138.
[20] Davids, 1 Peter, p. 175.

solidarity with other leaders was more important than an exalted title though he is named among 'the twelve.[21]

Peter then exhorts the elders to 'shepherd the flock among you, giving the oversight thereof.' The term 'oversight' is the same root term for bishop *(episkopeo)*. In effect, Peter tells the elders *(prebuteroi)* to function as bishops *(episkopoi)* over the flock of God.[22] Even though the church was embryonic and the nomenclature for pastor, elder, and bishop was often used interchangeably, the term apostle *(apostolos)* was not typically used in changeable ways with the other leadership designations for it connoted a different function within Christ's body. Peter's usage of this term indicates that Peter must have seen himself (though an apostle) functioning as a bishop whose responsibilities now included watchful oversight. At the very least, it indicates that Peter saw himself as an apostle with oversight (as a bishop) and did not see his colleagues as apostles but rather as bishops.[23]

Secondly, this passage reveals an important consideration for those who would serve as bishops in the Lord's church. As church pastors, elders (bishops), and leaders it must be understood that we are all on the same team. Peter ad dressed himself with respect to his colleagues as a 'fellow elder' *(sumpresbuteros)*. Though he could speak with special authority as an apostle of the Lamb, he chose the route of humility in creating collegial community with

---

[21] Grudem, 186,
[22] Ibid., p. 187.
[23] Davids, 1 Peter, pp. 177-178.

his fellow laborers in Christ.[24] The term 'fellow-elder is unique to the New Testament.[25] It is not found in other ancient Greek literature. This indicates that Peter himself probably coined the term in order to articulate the humble position that he assumed. Peter saw himself and encouraged other leaders to see themselves as co-laborers rather than competitors to the glory of God. He likely did this in light of the burgeoning brand of 'super-apostles' who were touting an exalted authority above 'the twelve,' the likes of whom Paul addressed in the Corinthian communication.

Finally, Peter warns the bishops/elders that *how* they lead the flock is equally as important as *that* they lead the flock. He insists that they should lead with vigor and enthusiasm, not by compulsion or slothfully.[26] He warns them against greed, turning ministry into commerce and seeking to minister for profit, which some were doing that early on in the life of the church.[27] He ultimately adjures them that they should not rule over the flock of God as taskmasters but rather as examples. He instructs them that bishops will have to give an account as to their oversight of the congregation.

Conclusion

---

[24] Hillyer, I and 2 Peter, p. 138
[25] Davids, 1 Peter, p. 176.
[26] Ibid., 180-182.
[27] Hillyer, pp. 139-140.

A bishop in the Lord's church as seen in sacred Scripture played a viable and important role within the church of the Lord Jesus Christ. From worship to doctrine, government to missions, the bishop in Scripture was and is a necessary officer for the survival and longevity of the church. As has been demonstrated in this chapter, the bishop is a scriptural office that commonly and frequently functioned in Christ's church. The church (grown out of its Jewish roots) prescribed the ecclesial (often hierarchical) structures that existed including the criterion, function, scope of authority, and sphere of rule of the bishops during the Apostolic Era. This chapter has endeavored to explore some biblical foundations for episcopal, church structure that can now be built upon to discuss episcopacy in the Patristic Period through at least two significant figures of church history. Chapter three will embark upon this exploration and provide historical insights into the development of the office of the bishop.

I Timothy 3 1-7

This is a faithful saying: If a man desires the position of a bishop, he desires a good work. ² A bishop then must be blameless, the husband of one wife, temperate, sober-minded, of good behavior, hospitable, able to teach; ³ not given to wine, not violent, not greedy for money, but gentle, not quarrelsome, not covetous; ⁴ one who rules his own house well, having his children in submission with all reverence ⁵ (for if a man does not know how to rule his own house, how will he take care of the church of God?); ⁶ not a novice, lest being puffed up with pride he fall into the same condemnation as the devil. Moreover, he must have a good testimony among those who are outside, lest he fall into reproach and the snare of the devil.

Titus 1:5-9

For this reason I left you in Crete, that you should set in order the things that are lacking and appoint elders in every city as I commanded you- ⁶if a man is blameless, the husband of one wife, having faithful children not accused of dissipation or insubordination. ⁷For a bishop must be blameless, as a steward of God, not self-willed, not quick-tempered, not given to wine, not violent, not greedy for money, ⁸but hospitable, a lover of what is good, sober-minded, just, holy, self-controlled, ⁹holding fast the faithful word as he has been taught, that he may be able, by sound doctrine, both to exhort and convict those who contradict.

I Peter 5: 1-4

The elders who are among you I exhort, I who am a fellow elder and a witness of the sufferings of Christ, and also a partaker of the glory that will be revealed: ²Shepherd the flock of God which is among you, serving as overseers, not by compulsion but willingly, not for dishonest gain but eagerly; 3 nor as being lords over those entrusted to you, but being examples to the flock; 4and when the Chief Shepherd appears, you will receive the crown of glory that does not fade away.

CHAPTER THREE

Apostles to Bishops: Historical and Theological Developments

Introduction

The progression of governmental leadership in the church from apostles to bishops is a fascinating and nuanced narrative. Historically, bishops succeeded the apostles in the work of ministry and the leadership of the church.[1] As has been seen in the Pauline and Petrine epistles and in the previous two chapters, the nomenclature, function, oversight, and some of the authority of the apostles, has shifted to the emerging leaders, the bishops. This was an important consideration and development to the fledgling church in light of the role the bishops played in defending orthodox doctrine. This transfer of authority was also important in that the blessedness of apostolic succession was entrusted to the recognized collegium of bishops in the face of the 'secret tradition' of the Gnostics.[2]

---

[1] Gonzalez, The Story of Christianity: Volume 1, pp. 65-66.
[2] Ibid. p. 66.

The historical tradition of the church testifies to the way church leadership evolved in the first century of the Christian era. The apostles were reported to have migrated from the Palestinian region into various parts of the world heralding the gospel and making bishops as they went. Church historians Scott Sunquist and Dale Irvin pen it thusly,

> The original twelve, according to later traditions, went to different regions of the world. Historical tradition remembers Thomas as having traveled to Edessa and India to the east, while Mark is remembered as evangelizing in Alexandria, and Matthew in Ethiopia. John most likely spent his last days in Asia Minor, while Peter and Paul were held by ancient tradition to have been executed in Rome. In each place where these apostles were said to have gone, early traditions identify bishops (or overseers) as their successors, maintaining a sense of connection with the original apostles.[3]

Most of the historians are clear and agreed that the work of apostles was entrusted to bishops and the title 'Apostle' was used less and less frequently to designate church leaders. Almost all reference to apostles in the first

---

[3] Dale T. Irvin and Scott W. Sunquist, History of the World Christian Movement Volume I: Earliest Christianity to 1453 (Maryknoll, New York: Orbis Books, 2009) p. 41 4 Ibid. p. 50

century through the third century was with reference to 'the twelve.'

Though there were many leaders who contributed greatly to the development of the episcopacy, this chapter will examine the lives and work of two key leaders who surfaced as primary theologians of the episcopacy during the Patristic Period. Those figures are Ignatius of Antioch and Cyprian of Carthage. As bishops, they were tasked with retaining, transmitting, and interpreting the life and ministry of Jesus to subsequent generations.' Thus, the office of the bishop had a specific function and a mammoth responsibility early in the second century through the early fourth century. The theology of this Apostolic Father (Ignatius) and this great North African theologian (Cyprian) has influenced the office and function of the bishop from the 2nd century forward.

Building upon the historical theological work of Justo L. Gonzalez, Dale T. Irvin, Scott W. Sunquist, Roger Olson, Bruce Shelley, et al, this chapter will explore the historical and theological development of the office of the bishop and trace some of its trajectories to the present. Special attention will be given to the theological emphasis of the patristic fathers (Ignatius and Cyprian) with a view to understanding their theological framework and ecclesiastical models. I am writing this chapter to expiate a well-rounded understanding of the progressive history from apostles to bishops, and a fully orbed understanding of the theology of the office of the bishop. In so doing, I expect that this research will inform the office and function of the bishop within the contemporary Pentecostal church while connecting the same to the historical moorings of this sacred office.

Statement of the Problem

Early church governmental structure evolved out of the need to promote the 'faith once delivered to the saints.' Birthed in a pluralist society, Christianity competed for its place in the culture along with many other religious sects.[4] The notion of 'catholicity' as proffered by Ignatius of Antioch in the early church spoke much more broadly to its doctrinal codification that only could happen through the collective voice of the universal church, 'according to the whole.'[5] In the absence of the canon of Scripture, the early church relied upon the Holy Spirit to superintend the process of doctrinal development and to protect the community from heresy and falsehood. In the first century the apostles were the vessels that the Holy Spirit used to relay the message of Christ.[6] Now in the second and third centuries, that responsibility had been passed to the bishops who were descendants (so to speak) of the apostles. They were tasked as theologians to construct doctrine from the narrative of Christ and His apostles. were the vessels that the Holy Spirit used to relay

---

[4] Ibid., 50.
[5] Bruce Shelley, *Church History in Plain Language*, Dallas, TX: Word Publishing, 1995, pp. 4-6.
[6] Gonzalez, The Story of Christianity, p. 66.

the message of Christ.[7] Now in the second and third centuries, that responsibility had been passed to the bishops who were descendants (so to speak) of the apostles. They were tasked as theologians to construct doctrine from the narrative of Christ and His apostles.

The primary doctrinal concern for the early church was refutation of the heretical teaching called 'Gnosticism'.[8] Though the Gnostics did not have a unifying theology, structure, or leadership, they believed that they possessed a special and higher spiritual knowledge than that of catholic faith.[9] Rather than the early church structure that sought the truth in the collective voices of the apostolic witness, Gnostics had various individual teachers, each with 'special' knowledge to transmit to waiting listeners. Their brand of spirituality fostered individual interpretation, spiritual elitism, division, and a fragmentation of the Christian community.[10]

The emergence and development of the episcopacy in the second century was in part the result of the rampant individualism of Gnostic spirituality and its injurious effect upon the fledgling Christian community.[11] Bishops were charged to preserve the unity of the church by maintaining the continuity of orthodox apostolic teaching and the connectedness of the universal versus local church.[12] They did so against the claims of Gnostics that their 'special' knowledge

---

[7] Shelley, p. 15.
[8] Olson, p. 28.
[9] Ibid., p. 29.
[10] Gonzalez, The Story of Christianity, p. 36.
[11] Shelley, p. 71.
[12] Ibid., p. 28.

came from the apostles as well.[13] The bishops were agents of remembrance and guardians of the great tradition of the church. Many of them wrote treatises defending the faith and narrating the stories of the various communities of faith.[14] All of this was done to preserve the unity of the fragile church in the face of diabolical doctrinal error being proffered by heretics. Thus, bishops became the symbol of the unity and doctrinal purity of the church.[15]

Influenced by the Gnosticism that was so prevalent in the second century, the unity of the church was threatened by the emergence of an individual voice seeking to supersede the collective orthodoxy of the whole church in the person of Montanus.[16] His work began as a well-intentioned, though heretically influenced, and thus misguided effort to reenergize the church with spiritual power and zeal. The challenge for Montanus was that his efforts stemmed from his belief that he was God's spokesperson sine qua non.'[17] He referred to himself as 'the mouthpiece of the Holy Spirit.[18] It was the Gnostic influence of individualism and access to 'special spiritual knowledge' that fostered the atmosphere for this type of hubris and spiritual practice. Likewise, it was the developing framework of the bishopric that stood in contrast to such heresy. The bishop embodied the salvific orthodoxy of the church as its leader and principal theologian.[19]

---

[13] Olson, p. 36.
[14] Gonzalez, *The Story of Christianity*, p. 41.
[15] Ibid., 97.
[16] Olson, 31-33.
[17] Ibid., p. 31.
[18] Ibid.
[19] Ibid., p. 36.

Ultimately, Montanus was labeled a heretic and forbidden to teach in the church.

The church's development of the episcopacy was also influenced by the preponderance of the question of sin, forgiveness, and restoration to the church and by the church.[20] In the second and third centuries, the church began to embrace the notion that the bishops (elders) could forgive sins and thus the episcopacy was crystallized around that episcopal prerogative (Jn 20:19-23).[21] It is interesting that the sin problem and the issues of forgiveness and restoration necessitated the advent of the bishopric to administer the means of grace for the forgiveness of those sins and for re-admittance to the Christian community. As we will see through the example of Cyprian, hamartiological issues were significant and often times controversial. Thus, they required the stewardship of a bishop for their resolution. The complexity of the issue of sin is illustrated in the second and third century church's understanding that three sins were thought to be pardonable by God but not by the church. Those sins were, sexual sins, murder, and apostasy. Crystallizing the governmental structure of the church to preserve its unity in the face of error, heresy, and sin was a paramount concern for early church fathers, leaders, and theologians. Two notable examples of church leaders, who were highly influential in the defense of the church, and the development of the episcopacy, now come to the fore.

---

[20]Gonzalez, The Story of Christianity, p. 67.
[21]Shelley, 69-70.

Ignatius of Antioch

After the turn of the first century, Ignatius of Antioch, a church father (and to some the third apostolic father), began in his correspondence to the churches in Asia Minor using a threefold ministry or a three-tier organizational structure for the church. In it he designates the bishop as the single highest office in the church.[22] He wrote these correspondences while in route to his impending demise in Rome.[23] In Ignatius' mind, bishops should labor as successors to the apostles who in Scripture were ruling, and governmental leaders. He strongly emphasized Christian obedience to the bishops. It is almost certain that he either knew some of the apostles or he was trained by the direct successors to the apostles.[24]

His seven letters to churches and individuals under his charge are highly influential for our understanding of the bishopric. They are not works of systematic theology but rather; they speak of refutation of false doctrine and in support of the unity of the church, the preservation of which, Ignatius sees as a function of the bishop.[25] Ignatius envisioned the church as one, unified, and whole. Thus, he was the first to proffer the term 'catholic' in his description of the church.[26] Although it took almost a whole century for this type of church government to take hold in the church at large,

---

[22] Ibid., p. 70-71.
[23] Gonzalez, History of Christian Thought, p. 71.
[24] Olson, p. 46.
[25] Ibid. p. 73.
[26] Ibid., p. x, see Shelley

Ignatius' die hard acquiescence to an episcopal form of government rings true in his writings and lays the foundation for our contemporary understanding of the episcopacy. Though he was not a constructive theologian, his works bear great importance for Christian theology in that they emphasize the fundamentals of the Christian faith and set the church on a trajectory toward orthodoxy.[27]

Ignatius codified the Lord's Supper into the celebration of the Eucharist and in so doing added theological weight and sacerdotal significance to its observance.[28] He understood the meal to have salvific efficacy toward those who partook of the bread and wine. He also understood the meal to be a part of the via saludus, the way of salvation. Foreshadowing Orthodox theology, Ignatius contended that observance of the Eucharist ushered the convert into the process of salvation later called theosis. This was the theological weight and depth that Ignatius brought to the episcopacy and that which he required from those who occupied that sacred office.

Ignatius built his theology of the episcopacy upon the person of Christ in the church most presently through the Eucharist. He saw the bishop as standing in persona Christi, in the stead of Christ, as the minister of the sanctuary. As Christ's representative, the bishop was the fountainhead of the Spirit and the principle theologian (interpreter of the apostolic memory) for that congregation or city. It was

---

[27] Ibid.,
[28] Olson, p. 46.

through this structure that evolved from the leadership of the apostles, that Ignatius led and instructed the church. His writings indicate that he was interested in preserving the unity and doctrinal fidelity of apostolic teaching, though he did not regard himself to be on par with the apostles.[29] The tenor of the times in which he lived required a 'firm hand' on the helm of the fledgling church.

Because the church was growing in an environment that was religiously pluralistic and, in some ways, turbulent, Ignatius found it necessary to assert some bold and even dogmatic statements concerning the bishopric. He did so in an attempt to preserve the unity of the church and the purity of apostolic memory.[30] In his letter to the church at Smyrna he wrote,

> You must all follow the bishop, as Jesus Christ followed the Father, and follow the presbytery as you would the apostles; respect the deacons as the commandment of God. Let no one do anything that has to do with the church without the bishop. Only that Eucharist that is under the authority of the bishop (or whomever he himself designates) is to be considered valid. Wherever the bishop appears, there let the congregation be; just as wherever Jesus Christ is, there is the catholic church. It is not permissible

---

[29] Ibid.
[30] Irvin and Sundquist, *World Christian Movement*, p. 6.

either to baptize or to hold a love feast without the bishop.³¹

To the Magnesian Christians, he wrote: "As the Lord did nothing without the Father, either by himself or through the apostles (for he was united with him), so you must not do anything without the bishop and the presbyters (elders)."³² To the Ephesians he wrote, "It is obvious, therefore, that we must regard the bishop as the Lord himself."³³ These statements arose from a pressing need to keep order in an increasingly diverse and unruly Christianity.³⁴

The order for which Ignatius strove and his strong conviction for the bishopric was for the purpose of keeping the church unified. He was concerned that the church maintained a unified memory of the testimony of Jesus and continuity of the apostolic tradition.³⁵ Though catholicity came to mean conformity to dogma and liturgy in later generations, in Ignatius' era catholicity was a relational proposition that required brother bishops to 'dwell together in unity.³⁶ Those relationships between bishops required mutual and consensual submission to one another, to catholic or orthodox theology, for the corporate preservation and advancement of the church. The bishopric began in unity, for the purpose of preserving unity, through the power of a unified memory of Jesus. Ignatius fortified the bishopric

---

[31] Ignatius, Letter to the Smyneans, 8, in Holmes, 190-191. ANF, 1:89.
[32] Ignatius, Letter to the Magnesiums 7, in Holmes, 155 in ANF, 1:62.
[33] Ignatius, To the Ephesians 7, Lightfoot, Harner and Holmes
[34] Olson. p. 47.
[35] Irvin and Sundquist, World Christian Movement, p. 66-67.
[36] Ibid.

because of the threat of outsiders who spoke of other apostolic interpretations and other apostolic traditions.[37]

His was an attempt to manage outsiders. The principle outsiders Ignatius was after were those who drifted from apostolic memory or orthodox teaching. This has been a central concern of bishops from the beginning of the episcopacy. Whether those outsiders were outside of the faith, or within the faith proclaiming false or heretical doctrines. As time went on the concern for outsiders extended to those who had been previously inside the household of faith but were now outside the church through excommunication and lapsarianism. With this concern at hand, another establishmentarian of the episcopacy now comes to the fore.

Cyprian of Carthage

Cyprian was the bishop of the important North African city of Carthage. Converted to the faith in his forties, he was consecrated a[38] bishop one year later.[39] His life and ministry had a tremendous impact upon the Christian faith and upon the structure of the church. He taught on the importance of the episcopacy and thus helped to crystalize the church's governmental structure for the next 1800 years.[40] Though he

---

[37] Ibid., 72.
[38] Gonzalez, The Story of Christianity, 88.
[39] Olson, p. 116.
[40] Ibid. p. 113.

was not a major theological voice, his impact upon the church was indelible and lasting. He has come to be known, as 'The most remarkable personality of the African church between Tertullian and Augustine.[41]

Born in the third century, Cyprian's life and ministry were encompassed about with the persecutions that befell the church during that period. Though he began his life worshiping the pagan Roman gods, his conversion landed him squarely in the middle of the persecution the church was experiencing.[42] The two principle Roman Emperors who brought superior levels of persecution during this period were Diocletian and Decius.[43] Decius directly impacted Cyprian's life and work with his insistence that all citizens of Carthage (a Roman city in North Africa) worship the Roman deity.[44] They could do so in connection to or alongside the worship of other 'gods', but they must offer allegiance to the Roman god. Cyprian resisted this notion and thus came into disfavor with Decius.

Cyprian linked an understanding of the unity of the church with personal salvation. For him, salvation began with and continued in fellowship within the church.[45] Cyprian believed that the process of salvation began at baptism, where the Holy Spirit was imparted through the laying on of the hands of the bishop and continued throughout one's life in

---

[41] Gonzalez, A History of Christian Thought, 238.
[42] Gonzalez, The Story of Christianity, 88-89.
[43] Olson, p. 115
[44] Gonzalez, The Story of Christianity, pp. 85-88.
[45] Olson, pp. 118-119.

the church. His vision of salvation was one of strict obedience to the commands of Christ.[46] Cyprian also conceptualized the church as being inextricably bound to the office of the bishop.[47] For him, without the bishop there would be no church.[48] In the Ante Nicene Fathers Cyprian says, 'You ought to know that the bishop is in the church and the church is in the bishop; and if anyone is not with the bishop, that he is not in the church… The church, which is catholic and one, is not cut nor divided, but is indeed connected and bound together by the cement of priests, who cohere with one another.[49]

For Cyprian, the unity of the church and thus the very possibility for salvation rested in the office of the bishop.[50] He understood the bishopric in Judaic terms as 'The office of our priesthood'[51] Thus, he perceived that the bishops, like priests, had the authority to forgive sins. His understanding of the bishopric was further expiated a century later in the Apostolic Constitutions, which paralleled the organizational structure of the Temple of the Jews with the church of the Lord Jesus Christ.[52] As the high priest carried a great deal of authority in the economy of Israel, so did the bishop in the third century church.[53] The bishop was seen as governor, priest, mediator,

---

[46] Ibid., p. 119.
[47] Greg Alison, *Historical Theology: An Introduction to Christian Doctrine*, (Grand Rapids, MI: Zondervan Publications, 2011), p. 592-592-593.
[48] Ibid., 593.
[49] Cyprian, Letter 68.8 in ANF, 5, 363.
[50] Allison
[51] Cyprian Letter 62.19 in ANF, 5, 363.
[52] Apostolic Constitutions 2.4.25 in ANF, 7, 410.
[53] Ibid., 2.3.20 in ANF, 7,404.

teacher of piety, keeper of knowledge, and father. He saw the bishop as the chief officer for the unity of the church.

Though Cyprian believed in a unified church he was not convinced of a monarchial episcopacy with one bishop ruling over all.[54] Rather, he contended that no bishop had the right to rule over another. He also strongly asserted that the bishops should be unified in their judgments and teaching. Cyprian showed a great deal of flexibility concerning customs and practices within the church. He did however reluctantly concede that the bishop of Rome (the bishop who would at a later point become the Pope) was the 'first among equals.'[55]

According to Cyprian, there were distinctive marks of a true bishop.[56] First, the bishop had to be ordained or consecrated by another bishop in good standing with the church.[57] Second, those who had received apostolic succession must recognize him as a legitimate bishop endowed with the spiritual gifts that belonged to the community of faith (the church) and the officials of the church and as one who teaches the truth faithfully.[58] Next, the bishop could not be a heretic. Also, a true bishop could not be self-appointed.[59] Finally, a true bishop could not separate himself from the fraternity of bishops and retain legitimacy.

---

[54] Gonzalez, *A history of Christian Thought*, 65-66.
[55] Olson, 121.
[56] Edward A. Englebrecht. The Church from Age to Age: A History from Galilee to Global Christianity. (St. Louis, MO: Concordia Publishing) 2011, 30-31.
[57] Ibid., 31.
[58] Olson, The Story of Christian Theology, 121.
[59] Ibid.

Roger Olson affirms this powerful notion thusly; 'Anyone who schismatic ally separates himself from the communion and fellowship of other bishops is a false bishop.[60]

Cyprian's ecclesiology is what Justo Gonzalez refers to as a 'federated view of the episcopate.[61] This meant that 'every bishop had a certain autonomy, although he must also listen to the fraternal recommendations of other bishops and must obey the decisions of a council.' This demonstrates Cyprian's affinity for fraternity[62] and his strident efforts toward maintaining the unity of the church. He saw the bishop not only as the symbol of the unity that was to be desired, but he also saw the bishop as unity's embodied reality. His contribution to the development of the episcopacy can still be discerned in the ecclesial structures that exist within the church today. A careful examination of those structures will reveal the potency and impact of Cyprian's episcopal leadership model.

Conclusion

By the late second century or the early third century the church was coming into stability and firmness with several major accomplishments. These accomplishments were recognized by the church and affirmed by the bishops of the church. Ignatius and Cyprian did much to guide the

---

[60] Ibid.
[61] Gonzalez, History of Christian Thought, p. 245
[62] Ibid.

church into that stable place and to defend the church from error and heresy. Their dogged theological efforts yielded much fruit from which the contemporary church benefits presently. Here are a few of the outcomes of the historical and theological development of the episcopacy over the second and third centuries.

The church discerned and discovered that the episcopal form of leadership (the bishopric) was in alignment with the leadership of the apostles. Even though the Christian movement had struggles and challenges both within and without, according to Dale Irvin and Scott Sunquist, 'By the end of the second century there was a general consensus among most of those who called themselves Christian that the major institutional structure of the movement was found in churches led by bishops, elders, and deacons, and that these churches stood in historical continuity with the original apostles of Jesus.' This insight frames the forthcoming observations[63] and assertions in chapters four and five within an historical framework that provides for analysis and critique.

Second, though the church was fraught with doctrinal and theological controversy in the early centuries, four flowers bloomed out of the chaos that would likely not have come forth had it not been for the doctrinal disparity. The first flower was the generation of the creeds of the church. The creeds were statements of the beliefs of the Christian community that were borne out of a need to succinctly

---

[63] Irvin and Sundquist, World Christian Movement, p. 49

articulate the Christian faith. They were baptismal confessions and theological statements of the divinity of Christ that served to catechize the church into an appropriate belief system.

The second flower was the canon of Scripture itself. Because some of the writings of the apostles and the evangelists were circulating throughout various Christian communities, there arose a need to codify the authentic writings that captured the apostolic memory and the words of our Lord. The process of the canonization of sacred Scripture gave the church its rule for faith and practice. This was accomplished under the leadership of the bishops.

The third flower that bloomed from controversy was the blessedness of apostolic succession. Arising out of a need to maintain orthodox spirituality, spiritual descendants of the apostles (the bishops) and of apostolic teaching were given the authenticating touch from a bishop within the lineage of the apostles to affirm their message and their legitimacy. Apostolic succession denoted a common faith shared by the growing Christian community. Its goal was to protect the church from heresy and the dangerous fruit of Gnostic individualism and super spiritual self-governance.

The final flower was the bishopric itself. Ignatius and Cyprian's efforts to crystalize a form of government that would serve, protect, and expand the church was realized in the episcopacy. Grounded in the leadership tradition of the Jews and born from the womb of the apostles, the bishops emerged to carry on the work begun by our Lord. Their charge was to stabilize the church and preserve the apostolic memory. This form of government has stood the test of time in the performance of this assignment for over one thousand eight hundred years.

Revelation 2:2 (NIV)

I know your deeds, your hard works and perseverance. I know that you cannot tolerate wicked people, that you have tested those who claim to be apostles but are not, and have found them false.

Revelation 2:2 (ESV)

I know your works, your toil and your patient endurance, and how thou cannot bear with those who are evil, but have tested those who call themselves apostles, and are not, and found them to be false.

CHAPTER FOUR

Contemporary Apostles: An Appreciation and Critique

Introduction

Since the 1990s, there has been resurgence in the recognition of the gift of the apostle.[1] That resurgence has typically been within Pentecostal and Charismatic circles. Though many persons with evangelical theological orientation have resisted the use of this nomenclature, the apostles have made a comeback. Cessationist theology has even called into question the legitimacy of the office of the apostle. They have questioned its appropriateness and usage for today. Because of the theological and historical connectedness between the apostle and the bishop, this chapter seeks to examine the contemporary expression of the gift of the apostle to discover its legitimacy and functionality within the contemporary church.

Building upon the work of Vinson Synan, John Eckhart, Ralph Dennis, C. Peter Wagner, et al, this chapter

---

[1] C. Peter Wagner, Wagner, Apostles and Prophets: The Foundations of the Church, (Ventura CA: Regal Books, 2000), p. 14.

will explore the claims of contemporary theologians and ministry practitioners concerning the gift of the apostle. Their work will be interrogated and placed in the historical theological light of the previous chapters. It will also be examined for its virtuous contributions to the contemporary theological landscape. The goal of this chapter is for readers to emerge with a more comprehensive understanding of and appreciation for the ministry, gift, and work of the apostle and the applicability that the functional designation, 'apostle' may have for today's church.[2]

I am writing this chapter from the perspective of a male, middle aged, Afro-Hispanic, Pentecostal, scholar/practitioner. I have been married to Dr. Antoinette G. Alvarado for twenty-three years and together we have three, teenage children. I have been a preacher of the gospel for thirty-eight of my fifty years of life. Over the twenty-three years of my pastorate, I have helped to plant at least ten churches by God's grace, and I continue to consult pastors and leaders on matters of church government and development. I was confirmed an apostle in June 2002 by my spiritual father, LaFayette Scales. In March 2005, the pastors that I served elected me the presiding bishop of the Grace Fellowship of Churches International. After a period of preparation, I was consecrated a bishop in the Lord's Church in June 2006.

I thought it necessary to provide some biographical information so that readers will be able to discern my vantage point and frame of reference. I have often found it helpful in

---

[2] Ibid., p. 22-23.

my own reading to know more about the author and to filter his or her claims through the grid of their experience, exposure, training, and theological orientation. I hope that you found this helpful as well.

This chapter is outlined according to the following sections. First, I will review some of the current literature on the apostolate from contemporary theologians and ministry practitioners. I will identify, describe, evaluate, and appreciate their works highlighting the aspects of their texts that most advances the conversation at hand. In the next section of this chapter, I will articulate an appreciation for their various contributions to the subject and to the contours of the landscape of the contemporary apostolate. I will expand on themes and issues that surface within the literature that I reviewed. In the third section, I will engage the notion of a contemporary apostolate from a critical, historical, biblical, and academic perspective. In so doing, I will draw on the resources of the academy, theology, and the church. This is in an attempt to critically analyze the validity and usefulness of the claims of contemporary theologians and practitioners who advocate for a contemporary apostolate. I will conclude this chapter with some final thoughts and questions for future study.

Literature Review

The purpose of this section is to examine the contemporary literature concerning the ministry and gift of the apostle. To this end I will survey four books drawing from each of them the salient points that contribute to the discussion at hand. Part of the reason for limiting my study to only four contemporary books is that the space for expiating my findings is limited. While the scope of this study is broad and the implications of this work are nuanced and vast, I will delimit the literature review to the most significant works of the contemporary period. For the sake of organization, I will proceed in chronological order of publication.

The book, *Apostles Prophets and the coming Moves of God,* by Dr. Bill Hamon, is an introduction to the ministry of apostles and prophets that forecasts trends that he discerns are on the horizon for the body of Christ. It is also a didactic text that seeks to instruct its readers in the ways of the Spirit by establishing apostles and prophets in their respective functions. In two hundred, ninety pages, Dr. Hamon addresses seminal Charismatic themes of apostles and prophets, their ministries, and predictive statements concerning the future of apostolic and prophetic ministry, and the future of the church. Published on Destiny Image Publishers in 1997, this text was one of the earlier contemporary monographs on the subject of apostles.

Apostles Prophets and the Coming Moves of God, is divided into eighteen chapters with significant front matter and afterword. Complete with a glossary of apostolic and prophetic terms and a section with resources for continued growth in this area of study, this text seeks to be fully orbed in its presentation of all things prophetic and apostolic. The broad range of chapters in this text cover various topics of interest to Pentecostal Charismatic Christians. From the opening chapter entitled, 'What is Happening Now?' (pp. 7-22), to a chapter on the biblical perspective of an apostle Dr. Hamon engages the subject with sincerity and zeal. He addresses themes of doctrinal development in the chapter entitled, 'Apostles and Church Doctrine' (pp. 43-50) and pushes back against theological excesses in chapter twelve called, 'Extremes in the Restoration of Truth' (pp. 189-210).

Written in the vernacular, this text is an introductory contribution to the apostolate and the ministry of the prophet. It is formatted clearly and thus it is easy to move from chapter to chapter. As a matter of fact, it reads as though one might be reading through sermon transcriptions. Dr. Hamon's literary style is colloquial and expressive. There is nothing overly ambitious about the vernacular used in this text thus, it seems to have been written for laypersons and clergy alike.

Apostles Prophets and the Coming Moves of God, has several dimensions that I greatly appreciate. Its readability makes it accessible to a broad range of readers. Dr. Hamon covers a wide range of topics in the text that make it a good reference for terms and issues within the Pentecostal Charismatic orbit. He is courageous in his prophetic assertions, making predictions boldly and convincingly.[3] His prophetic imagination envisions the future under God's rule, which expresses a modified 'Kingdom Now,' 'Finished Work'

---

[3] Bill Hamon, *Apostles Prophets and the Coming Moves of God,* (Shippensburg, PA: Destiny Images, 1997), p. 6.

theology.[4] He also endeavors to provide scriptural support for the vast majority of his claims. As I read this text, I get a strong sense of Dr. Hamon's fidelity to the text of Scripture, and that is to be commended.

I am, however, concerned with the fact that there is hardly any reference to church history other than biblical history mentioned in this text. Dr. Hamon seems to leap over one thousand nine hundred years of church history in order to capture a biblical vision of the apostolate. While I believe that it is important to ground theological concepts in scriptural moorings, I also think we do ourselves a disservice when we do not consult the witness of history. Articulating the historical context of the passage that he was using could have made his argument stronger.

For example, while making a valid point concerning apostles having different assignments. He warned his readers not to pigeonhole all apostles into the same functional mold. Dr. Hamon then used the obscure foundational apostles as examples of the fact that we do not know how God used them because there is no biblical history recorded. While this is true, if he would have appealed to church history, he could have illustrated his point more clearly by stating what the historical record said concerning their ministries that were not recorded in the text of sacred Scripture. This would have strengthened the point that he was making concerning God's sovereign use of his apostles. Dr. Hamon's refusal to include

---

[4] Ibid., p. 148.

church history as a part of his study while not 'wrong' is certainly limiting.

Overall, this text makes the ambitious leap toward developing a practical theology of the apostolate, but it seems to be inadequate on matters of theological substance and some questions of biblical accuracy. While it is almost certainly innocuous, Dr. Hamon's lack of depth and nuanced treatment of the broad themes of the apostolate make his work valuable as an entrée into the subject, but needful of a more robust historical, and theological framework.

John Eckhardt's, *Moving in the Apostolic: God's Plan to Lead His Church to the Final Victory* is an ambitious installment outlining God's strategy for the restoration of the apostolate in the twenty-first century. It is a quick read of only one hundred thirty-five pages divided into ten chapters that traverse the gamut of biblical topics beginning with a question on the mission of the apostle,[5] through the Blueprint for Apostolic Living.[6] It is light but provocative. Using a recurring 'Mission Impossible' motif, Apostle Eckhardt lays out his argument in a strategic way. It seems that he is interested in provoking his readers to action rather than impressing them with his knowledge.

Moving in the Apostolic does a good job of explaining to its readers what the term apostle means and who the

---

[5] John Eckhardt, *Moving in the Apostolic: God's Plan to Lead the Church to the Final Victory*. (Grand Rapids, MI: Chosen Books, 1999), p. 17.
[6] Ibid., 20.

apostles were.[7] Apostle Eckhardt also encourages his readers to embrace their calling and in this case to embrace their being sent as a sign of God's hand and favor on their lives. He expresses his affinity for the ministry of the apostles and sees that ministry living on through the church, which he calls apostolic (if they are living under the anointing of the apostles).[8] Finally, he connects the call to ministry that is upon the whole body of Christ with the call of God on the apostle.[9]

There are very few extra-biblical reference made in this text. It seems that Apostle Eckhardt is trying to remain biblically faithful and scripturally grounded. He uses many scriptures to advance his argument. For example, With reference to the 'apostolic spirit' he invokes John 14:26.[10] Again, he parallels the Holy Spirit with an apostolic spirit invoking John 20:21-22.[11] The biblio-centrism with which he advances his argument will be refreshing for many of the Pentecostal Charismatic audiences he will encounter. There is a strong focus on the Bible as the book for faith and practice among Pentecostals.

I appreciate Apostle Eckhardt's assertion that apostles are in many ways missionaries. His view that, 'Apostles were commanded by the Lord and set to be a light to the Gentiles (nations),[12] connects with my own missionary

---

[7] Ibid., 23.
[8] Ibid., p. 26.
[9] Ibid., p. 24.
[10] Ibid.
[11] Ibid., p. 25.
[12] Ibid., p. 39

zeal. For Apostle Eckhardt, in order for one to walk in the apostolic anointing, one must be prepared to take the gospel and apostolic witness to the ends of the earth.[13] He contends that the apostolic anointing will give the apostle authority to operate in territory that the Holy Spirit will give him.

In general, though Apostle Eckhardt's text is well intentioned to activate apostles for the twenty-first century, he makes some leaps of logic that are inaccurate and undermine the strength of the book. His assertion that the church as early as the second and third centuries 'drifted into ceremonialism and tradition' is inaccurate.[14] Likewise, his assertion that 'apostles are officers of the church'[15] has no basis in Bible, history, or tradition of the church. Again, his assertion that' Apostolic ministry operates at a rank high enough to speak on behalf of heaven[16] is not only unfounded in the Bible, it promotes some of the very things that the Bible warns against in terms of making ourselves Lords over one another instead of servants. When a Christian aspires to elevate in 'rank' it seems to me to be carnal and worldly. Apostle Eckhardt's advocacy for the same undermines what I believe he is trying to achieve in writing this text.

As I read the text, I genuinely got the sense that Apostle Eckhardt strongly believes his claims about apostolic ministry. His conviction resonates throughout, and this is good. His polemic against the church's acquiescence to

---

[13] Ibid.
[14] Ibid., p. 30.
[15] Ibid., p. 32.
[16] Ibid., p. 43.

culture and over reliance on tradition was refreshing. Though I was hoping to read his comments on whether there was any connection between apostles and bishops, I was disappointed to find none.[17] I was however encouraged to see the criterion for apostles that Apostle Eckhardt outlines in his text.[18] I trust that the spirit in which I made my comments will be understood and received as critical but irenic, corrective, and maybe even in the likeness of an apostle.

Dr. C. Peter Wagner's instructive text, *Apostles and Prophets, the Foundation of the Church* is an interesting and informative read. Written in just eight chapters, his work clarifies the ministry of apostles and prophets in ways that demystify and give clarity to long held questions. One hundred forty pages plus an index make it manageable for busy professional theologians to read in one or two settings. It is valuable to the church because it describes the calling, ministry, and function of apostles for the church today.

Chapter one reveals Dr. Wagner's notion of what the foundation of the church really is. Dr. Wagner argues that this foundation is Jesus.[19] He then quickly segues into Paul's scriptural assertion that the church is built upon the foundation of the apostles and prophets. So, in addition to Jesus being the foundation, Dr. Wagner takes seriously the claim that the apostles and prophets are part of the foundation as well.[20] This is the premise of the entire book.

---

[17] Ibid., p. 83-84.
[18] Ibid., p. 89-90.
[19] Wagner, pp. 5-6.
[20] Ibid., 6-7.

The rest of his argument throughout is based upon this foundational truth.

Chapters two and three explain what the apostle has to work with and how the apostles operate. From anointing to gifting, character to call, apostles have to work in the field where they are assigned and to work with the tools they have been given. Chapter three explains what categories of apostles Dr. Wagner sees in the church today. The four types of apostles that he lists; Vertical Apostles, Horizontal Apostles, Hyphenated Apostles, Marketplace Apostles, are interestingly defined and creatively included in the leadership matrix of the church.

Chapters four through six identify the needs, knowledge, and know-how that prophets and apostles require in order to co-labor as a team of servants. Dr. Wagner rightly reveals this concept of 'ministry pairing' as being God's way as was expressed in the early church. This means that ministry gifts like the apostle have complementary components and partners in ministry who synergize their efforts to do the will of God. This requires mutual submission and mutual accountability. Dr. Wagner advocates for the apostles to operate with that type of submission and accountability.

Chapters seven and eight culminate the text asserting that synergy between the prophet and the apostle is the design of God and the most effective means for prevailing in spiritual warfare. He offers testimonies[21] of his own journey having received prophecies from men and women who have clarified the direction that God was leading him through prophecy. The final chapter illustrates how he, as an apostle, has been a benefit and blessing to the prophets in his life circle.

There is much to be appreciated in this text. It is well-written, illustrated with testimony (which is very Pentecostal and appeals to the Pentecostal soul), and supported with some citations and documentation. It also needs to be said that Dr. Wagner is the main advocate and the primary voice in the modern movement toward the apostolate. Therefore, his words and teaching heavily influence most of the other contributors to this movement. Reading his works as a part of this study provides the foundation for the propositions of many of the other adherents of this sect of Christendom.

My only critique of this text is common to the writings of the leaders of this modem advocacy for the apostolate. Much of Dr. Wagner's biblical work, like his colleagues, has only a little critical exegetical component to it. He and others in this movement seem to have an affinity for the classical Pentecostal plain reading of Scripture method. As I was preparing to read his books for this study, I was anticipating more of a scholarly polish from him than from the others. This is not to disparage the other contributors to this literature review. I am only saying that I see Dr. Wagner as

---

[21] Ibid., 108-110.

scholar/practitioner whose reputation for scholarship preceded him.

Bishop Ralph L. Dennis' book, *Divine Distinction: The Ministry of the Apostle, The* Office of the Bishop, is a comparative analysis between the gift of apostle and the office of the bishop. Concisely written in sixty-seven pages, Bishop Dennis tackles one of the perennial ecclesiological challenges of the modern era amongst Pentecostal Charismatic Christians. In six brief chapters, Bishop Dennis defines the major issues and players, and then offers what he calls, 'The Simple Difference' in chapter five.[22] In his essay, Bishop Dennis argues for the necessity of seeing these two ecclesial designations (apostle and bishop) as functionally distinct, historically misunderstood, and ecclesially misappropriated. The corrective that he offers is helpful but does present some challenges.

One of the main challenges to Bishop Dennis' remedy is the absence of historical context for the functionality of the apostle and the bishop. While there is word play, and biblical reference, Bishop Dennis does not provide an historical frame-work that his readers might understand the historical development of either of the two designations (apostle and bishop) within the church. Without that context, there can be no nuanced understanding of the functional reality of the history of effects. The lack of historical context is what keeps

---

[22] Ralph L. Dennis, Divine Distinction: The Ministry of the Apostle, The Office of the Bishop. (Baltimore, MD: Xulon Press, 2002, pp. 55-62.

the church perpetually in 'first-century' mode, when the train of history has moved on to another era.

Though he appeals heavily to sacred Scripture, he is not addressing an exclusively or even principally a scriptural or interpretive issue. The concern for distinguishing between apostles and bishops is as much a historical/theological concern as it is a biblical concern. Obviously influenced by C. Peter Wagner, Bishop Dennis' work recapitulates many of the themes taken up by Dr. Wagner. Bishop Dennis also subscribes to the 'tiered' designation of apostles that Dr. Wagner proffers in his earlier publication.[23]

An Appreciation

There are several things that I appreciated about the apostolic movement. First, most of the authors whose books I read demonstrated a genuine desire to live out a biblical Christianity. All of the texts I reviewed have a strong biblical affinity and a real sense of fidelity to sacred Scripture. In my experience, this quality is becoming less and less common within the ranks of church leaders and ministry gifts. Since these authors are representatives of the 'new' apostolic movement, their adherence to sacred Scripture is encouraging.

Each contributing author seemed to be open to the Spirit of God and the Spirit's activity in the world today. By

---

[23] Ibid.

the very nature of the subject under discussion today I surmised that my dialogue partners are not cessationist. All of them attested to the fact that the Spirit of God is alive and active in the church and in the world, beckoning men and women unto salvation and getting the church ready to lead as the Kingdom of God expands and advances in the earth. Their affirmation that 'the wind blows where it listeth', meaning that the spirit is active, was encouraging to me.

Another aspect of these author's writings that I appreciated greatly was the fact that they are restorationist. They seek to live fully into the ongoing activity of the gifts and offices of the Spirit, alive and operant today. This is not common in all ecclesiastical circles. But it seems to me that within the Pentecostal Charismatic orbit, where this resurgence of apostles is more strongly in operation, there is a great desire to see the power of God manifested in the earth as a disruption to the works of the enemy.

They acknowledge the necessity for ministry partnership between apostles and prophets and ostensibly between other spiritual collaborators.[24] I was encouraged that all of the authors I read as a part of this study advocated for a team approach to ministry. This demonstrates their catholicity and consensual nature and connects them with the broader Christian tradition. They all acknowledged that team ministry; particularly between apostles and prophets was an authentic expression of the ministry of Christ in the earth.

---

[24] Eckhardt, p. 40

They all seem to have a missional orientation and operate from a strong sense of being 'sent' by God into the world.[25] This is noteworthy and important. As quiet as it might be kept, it appears to me that too much of what is being argued in this type of discussion is veiled vanity and desire for titles. The missional and functional dimension of apostles and bishops needs to be elevated to the fore and given pride of place. The authors of the texts that contributed to this chapter seem to share a burden for the lost, the expansion of the Kingdom of God, and the *missio dei*.

A Critique

The notion of contemporary apostles and the modern apostolate movement is not without shortcomings. I believe that the movement can benefit from healthy dialogue with those from other camps. Here are some of my concerns for this movement. The authors and progenitors of this movement seem to theologize from an ahistorical perspective of the church. This makes them all appeal to the 'good old (biblical) days' when the church had power. To their credit the authors[26] of these texts appealed heavily to the text of Scripture as their source. However, they did so to the diminution of history. They did not take into account the development of the church beyond the biblical narrative. They often demonstrated naive myopathy that precluded them from seeing the broader contextual and historical factors that

---

[25] Ibid., p. 21.
[26] Ibid., p. 17.

influenced the decision-making and function of the church. Too often they painted with a broad brush over issues that really required nuanced, detailed attention.

The ahistorical natures of their claims gives occasion for these leaders to theologize yet have no clear and discernable theological tradition or stream out of which this movement flows. In other words, there is a general sense of evangelical conservatism that I can detect in the readings. But it has no commitments beyond the Scripture itself. While some would say that this is a good thing, I contend that to theologize in this way means to do so without an historical community of interpreters to guide ones interpretation of the text of Scripture. One cannot even have a frame of reference to faithfully critique his or her own tradition if one is not aware of the camp or lenses through which one interrogates and interprets the text.

Some of its leaders or at least front-runners seem to be biblically and theologically uninitiated. A great deal of the biblical exegesis in these texts is wanting to say the least. Some of their treatment of the text has not been undergirded by careful study of Scripture in context and (where necessary) in the language of the day. The movement for the restoration of apostles would benefit greatly from a more nuanced study of the text of Scripture. This would shed greater light on the matter and allow for more critical engagement with the issue at hand.

There is too much comparison to the foundational apostles as if contemporary apostles are on par with them.

This gives the movement a quasi-gnostic feel, relying upon 'special knowledge' or insight that is only given by 'revelation' to the leaders of one's tribe or sect. With the exception of Bishop Dennis, most of the other contributors made the apostles of the churches on par with the apostles of the Lamb. Finally, even though they are forming apostolic networks, I am concerned that they seem to be populated by those who do not share theological convictions concerning the church and thus, they stagnate the advancement of the church. They advocate connectedness and solidarity, but they organize around the same 'free church' ethos that values independence and personal freedom over community.

Conclusion

Over the last few pages I have endeavored to present an affirmation and critique of the movement for contemporary apostles. I have sought to be fair and thorough, as much as one can be given the time and space concerns. I have reviewed some of the literature that informs the movement and considered some of the nuanced positions that members of that camp have taken. I have disclosed my personal position and given an auto-ethnographic disclaimer so as to remind myself to be impartial and unbiased to the degree that this is possible. It is my hope that you the reader have gleaned some benefit from these musings and can find applicability to your own life and ministry.

Ephesians 4:11a

And He Himself gave some to be apostles...

I Corinthians 15:5 – 7

And that He was seen of Cephas, then of the twelve: After that, He was seen of above five hundred brethren at once; of whom the greater part remain unto this present, but some are fallen asleep. After that, He was seen of James; then of all the apostles.

2 Corinthians 12: 12

Truly the signs of an apostle were wrought among you in all patience, in signs, and in wonders, and mighty deeds.

Galatians 3: 1

Paul, an apostle, (not of men, neither by man, but by Jesus Christ, and God the Father, who raised him from the dead)

Revelation 2:2

I know thy works, and thy labour, and thy patience, and how thou canst not bear them which are evil: and thou has tried them which say they are apostles, and are not, and hast found them liars:

CHAPTER FIVE

Concluding Thoughts: Responses to Common Questions and Critiques

Concluding Thoughts

For two thousand years the church has carried on the mission of Christ thus, apostles and bishops have been and continue to be important for doctrinal development and the practical life of the church. The church of Jesus Christ faces many challenges as she lives out her call in the world today. She is charged with the task of being a light in a darkened world bringing life and hope to those who are perishing. She carries the burden of being a spiritual and moral compass to the larger society. Her ministries are the hands of Christ extended in love to a world, which is hungry and perishing. She is also the city of refuge for those who have been disenfranchised by life and marginalized by political systems, powerful spirits, and personal scandals. Throughout the centuries, apostles and bishops have stewarded the church in performing these restorative acts of love and edification.

The church's history is laden with attempts to form and reform her tenets to be consistent with Scripture and compliant to the ever-speaking voice of God in the here and now. Some of the main interpreters of the voice of God and spokespersons from the beginning of ecclesial history have been the apostles and bishops. The church's various divisions and factions have often made it difficult to pin down what are the best practices for these ministry gifts, but the church's resolve has been for the 'unity of the faith, in the bond of peace' for which apostles and bishops have been of paramount importance. The church's numerous councils and conclaves led by the bishops have wrestled with the quantum of choices to be made and have proven necessary in order to discover what God desired to express through the church.

The principle concern that I have had for the contemporary church, and one of the main impetuses for writing this book has been to explore her belief systems, ecclesiology, government, and theological positions as it pertains to the ministry of the apostle and the office of the bishop. As I stated in the introduction, orthodoxy is a word that has in some ways been demonized within contemporary circles of Christian witness. It has been assigned meaning that to some is passé and restrictive. Though the term and tenets of orthodoxy are not widely promulgated in Pentecostal/Charismatic circles, I believe that the Pentecostal church should take a more profound look and intentionally reinvigorate the concept of orthodoxy within their various communities. To do so would almost certainly insist that the ministry of the apostle and the office of the bishop be reexamined and reconstituted.

Because there is so much injurious and erroneous doctrine being proffered in the larger sects of Christendom, I have been increasingly concerned with making the perpetuation of orthodoxy one of the main tenets of our episcopal leadership. As a bishop in the Lord's church, I have sought to engage in, understand, promote, live, and teach orthodox principles of Christian life, as I understand them through Scripture, scholarship, common witness, history, and community. The churches that I serve and the ministerial students that I teach have need of being acquainted with and oriented to higher standards of living as it pertains to godliness and Christian commitment.

In my opinion, there seems to be a misalignment of values in the larger society that has crept into the contemporary church, which has caused many of our congregants and even our colleagues to careen off course into worldly practices and godless affections. The inconsistency of the mixed messages of contemporary Christianity is in some ways undermining our ability to shepherd the flock of God with clear distinctions between the authentic and the disingenuous. The inordinate desire that many have for prosperity and possessions is unseating classical understandings of the Christian faith in favor of a gospel which promises much but requires little. This is for me a clarion call to reexamine the apostles' doctrine and appeal to the stewardship of bishops for sanity and stability in these unstable times.

The church throughout the ages has struggled with some of the same concerns, which you and I grapple with today.[1] Issues of doctrine and orthodoxy which includes concerns for church governance, authority, scriptural emphases, piety, worship, racism, baptism, and contextualization are but a few of the common themes which have been recapitulated throughout the ages in the church of God. The predominant way that the church has dealt with these matters seems to have been consistent from period to period. When the leaders of the church were in a quandary over new and/or difficult issues within the life of the church, the apostles (in the apostolic period) and bishops (throughout the rest of church history) often met in conclave to discuss matters of faith and practice (Acts 15).

Councils, synods, conferences, symposia, congresses, summits, and convocations are all descriptive of the ways the church has gathered to determine the mind, will, and disposition of God on various matters pertinent to the faith. These gatherings were first mentioned in the book of Acts and carryon to the present with similar consequence. The tridactic relationality between the word, the Spirit, and the community[2] seems to be the preferred method of discerning the purposes and intent of God for the people as it is recorded in sacred Scripture and practiced by the early bishops in the Lord's church. It seems to me that since the apostles and

---

[1] Shelly, pp. 99-101.
[2] Kenneth J. Archer, A Pentecostal Hermeneutic for the Twenty-first Century: Scripture, Spirit and Community. New York: T & T Clark, International, 2004.

bishops led that effort then, they should take part in doing so now. Today, we have the unique opportunity to look back upon the synodic meetings of the past in order to extract wisdom to address some of the contemporary issues that the church faces with ancient solutions.

The purpose for this inquiry is to discover some of the pillars of truth concerning apostles and bishops and their significance to the government, doctrine, and function of the church. It is in the discovery of this all-too-important substratum that we can begin to undergird the church with practices and policies that have both biblical and historical witnesses. This type of reflective inquiry will provide the church with the moorings necessary to be relevant, sanctified, orthodox, and fertile. Our thoughtful, spiritual, dialogical engagement with this text and with each other on the subject of apostles and bishops gives us the potential to nurture a church that will be counter-cultural and missional.

I am by no means suggesting that there can be no fresh or contemporary inspiration for innovative ways of doing and being the church in the 21st Century, or that we must exclusively appeal to history as our model. But what I am asserting is the notion that all of those novelties of 'modernity' broadly conceived be rooted in the text of sacred Scripture and grounded in the historical precedent that has been established by the early church. This is to say that many of the injurious doctrines, or dogmas, or practices, or ideologies, which have surfaced today, have actually resurfaced from previous periods in ecclesiastical history. Many have already either been affirmed or rejected by the church and need little or no attention. They simply need to be scanned through the filter of history to determine their authenticity. As leaders in the church we must be the ones who stand as watchmen on the wall.

Though there are many councils and conclaves, which deserve our investigation, I would like to focus on two. These two produced a statement and commentary on the nature of the church, which has guided her through one thousand six hundred years of Christendom. Those councils were the council of Nicaea (325 AD) and the council of Constantinople (381 AD). It was from these two gatherings of leaders that the Nicene Creed was developed and instituted as a doctrinal statement of belief for the church.[3] I have included the entire statement that was produced though we will examine only one of its phrases. As you read it please notice the biblical allusions or direct quotes from Scripture and the emphasis on the term 'one.'

---

[3] Olson, pp. 154-160.

We believe in one God,

the Father, the Almighty,

maker of heaven and earth,

of all that is seen and unseen.

We believe in one Lord, Jesus Christ,

the only Son of God,

eternally begotten of the Father,

God from God, Light from Light,

true God from true God,

begotten, not made, one in Being with the

Father.

Through him all things were made.

For us men and for our salvation

he came down from heaven:

by the power of the Holy Spirit

he was born of the Virgin Mary, and

became man.

For our sake he was crucified under Pontius Pilate;

he suffered, died, and was buried.

On the third day he rose again

in fulfillment of the Scriptures;

he ascended into heaven

and is seated on the right hand of the Father.

He will come again in glory

to judge the living and the dead, and his

kingdom will have no end.

We believe in the Holy Spirit, the Lord,

the giver of life,

who proceeds from the Father (and the Son).

With the Father and the Son he is worshipped

and glorified.

He has spoken through the Prophets.

We believe in one holy catholic and apostolic Church.

We acknowledge one baptism for the

forgiveness of sins.

We look for the resurrection of the dead,

and the life of the world to come. Amen.

Though there are many important things that are resolved and present in this creed, the one phrase that we will examine carefully will be the definitive credo on the nature, constitution, and existence of the church. That statement is consequential and deserves special attention. Its implications are far-reaching and give the church language to articulate the true nature of the ecclesial community (as understood by the apostles and bishops) in the light of the nebulous and often enigmatic contemporary church and in the wake of some current ecclesiastical practices, which seem questionable. That phrase that captures our attention today is, "We believe in one, holy, catholic, and apostolic Church."

The four tenets espoused in this statement seem to be the essential areas of emphases of the bishops as they set forth this treatise on the nature of the Christian life and an understanding of the church. Each of the four has implications for the contemporary church as we revision what it means to be aligned biblically and historically with the mission, intent, and purpose of God for the church of the Lord Jesus Christ. The purpose for highlighting these is to accentuate the theological emphases of bishops as they consider the weightier matters of the faith and the concerns of the church. In so doing, we may bore down to the gestalt of what the church should espouse and the interrelatedness of the ministry of the apostle in antiquity and the office of the bishop presently.

The starting point for understanding the church in light of these four axioms is to reiterate the notion that the church belongs to the Lord Jesus Christ and is a reflection of His inner-Trinitarian, social dynamism. The church is one because the Godhead is one; the church is holy because Jesus Christ is holy; the church is catholic because Jesus is the savior of all people, in every place, for all times; the church is apostolic because God sent Jesus into the world, Jesus sent the Holy Spirit into the world, and there is an inextricable bond between the legitimate ambassadors (apostles) and successors (bishops) of the message of the cross and Christ Himself.

The oneness of the church is expressed in the oneness of Jesus who is the Christ. 'That is to say, there is one place and one place only where we may stand and call God "Father." One place and one place only where that participation in the divine life which we hear of in 2nd Peter, which was referred to this morning, becomes a reality.'[4] The church is one in that it reflects the oneness of the Godhead though manifested in three persons or in the case of the church many branches (John 15:4). The church is one because it has but one savior and one means of salvation. In the first century, the apostles heralded that oneness as a tenet of the Christ-Church relationship. After that and still today, the bishops are the symbols of that oneness or unity within the church.

The church is not one in the sense that there are no divisions or schisms or factions. As with any entity that has experienced the influence of human intervention the church

---

[4] The Archbishop of Canterbury, Address to the Third Global South to South Encounter" Red Sea, Egypt, October 25, 2005.

is not perfectly unified in practice and/or expression. But, the unifying factor for the church, the thing that produces her oneness is the person of Christ in whom the church is found and the presence of the one true Spirit of life which binds all of its constituents together. The church is one because all of its members are found in Jesus Christ. There is no personal merit necessary to enter into the Church. There is only access by the one saviour. There is no alternate door or secondary entrance into this blessed communion. All who enter do so by the blood of the crucified Lamb of God who is Jesus the Christ. This produces the oneness, which the apostles affirmed as the initial ideology of the church and the bishops preserved as the nature of the church.

Sacred Scripture establishes the oneness of the church in that Paul teaches: 'There is one body and one spirit, just as you were called to the one hope that belongs to your call, one Lord, one faith, one baptism, one God and Father of us all' (Eph 4:4-5). In the Eucharist we all partake of the one bread. Jesus describes himself as the one 'good shepherd' (Jn 10:11). The Old Testament witness in Deuteronomy testifies that the 'Lord is one' (Deut 6:4). There seems to be a tenor of understanding throughout the witness of Scripture that Christ's desire is that His people understand that to be in communion with He and the Father through the Spirit means to be one with each other (Jn 17).

The church is also marked by the tenet of holiness. The moral authority of the bishop is buttressed by the personal holiness that he or she espouses and the corporate holiness with which the church functions. This descriptive attribute of the positional and practical reality of the church is often understated in the times in which we live. There is quite often little to no conversation public ally and/or privately about the holiness of God, the holiness of the bishop, the holiness Christ's church, and His expectation for a holy people. Though this was historically (in many circles) a celebrated and often over realized assertion, it has been to a large degree swallowed by the quagmire of what some Christians would call 'religious' or 'traditional.'

Historically, the Pentecostal movement has been a holiness movement. It has roots in the Wesleyan-Holiness tradition.[5] which emphasizes living with purity and integrity with God and man. Early on in the Pentecostal movement (particularly within the Afro-Pentecostal churches), leaders of the movements chose to use the title 'bishop' rather than 'apostle' as the chief progenitor of the holiness of their respective stream of Pentecostalism.[6] This tradition, with some variations between the different Pentecostal camps, was the precursor to the more modem Pentecostal/Charismatic movement. Understanding this holiness tradition is the necessary precursor to understanding the nature of the Pentecostal community's

---

[5] Stanley M. Horton and Gary B. McGee. Systematic Theology: A Pentecostal Perspective. Springfield, MO: Legion Books, 1994, pp. 10-11.

[6] Ithiel Clemmons, *Bishop C. H. Mason and the Church of God in Christ*. Lanham, MD: Pneuma Life Publications, 1996.

tradition of holy living and the bishop as the symbol of that holiness.

The culture that was created in the holiness societies of John Wesley was communal in nature.7 He understood the Christian life in terms of its communal dimensions. I am firmly persuaded that in addition to the Wesleyan influence that shapes modern Pentecostalism,8 there is also a view of the social Trinity, which can be helpful in informing our view of community and of holiness. As the Trinity of God relates with each other, so Pentecostals must model that type of holy, communal interaction. In other words, how a person views the community of God, in both social and economic Trinitarian interaction, will determine and or impact how that person will operate within the social constructs of the localized body to which he or she belongs. This is why the bishop, though the symbol of unity operates in confraternity with other bishops toward the mutual goals of establishing and advancing the Kingdom of God. How that outworking is demonstrated within each communion varies, but suffice it to say that as the bishop is the symbol of the oneness of the church, the bishop is the steward of the holiness of the church.

It needs to be understood that holiness has at least two major out-workings. They two are personal holiness, and communal holiness. These two work in tandem and are

---

[7] Olson, pp. 515-517
[8] Donald Dayton, The Theological Roots of Pentecostalism. Waco, TX: Baker Academic, 1987

two sides of the same proverbial coin. The community is only holy as the people who make up the community live in holiness. Likewise, personal holiness must be understood and realized by means of the whole community to which that individual belongs. Though this seems to be an unnecessary inclusion, it has been my experience that the requisite for the people of God to be holy has in many Christian's minds been diminishing steadily in the wake of contemporary accommodations for ungodly behavior. Jesus Christ established the church not only for the redemption of sinners but also for the sanctification of sinners. It is a necessary aspect of the mission of the church to facilitate the sanctification of her converts to a new way of being in the world. That new way is a holy way.

This is not to say that the church is holy because of its own merit, works, or posture. Rather, the church is holy because the author of the church is holy. The holiness of the church is a positional holiness that finds its fulfillment in practical ways of being in the world. In other words, a genuine born-again experience (positional relocation) will bring about a new way of living in the earth (practical expression). The church has been endowed by its progenitor with the sacramental means by which to help foster holiness within the lives of her constituents.

It is through the preaching of the word of God and the administration of the sacraments that the church 'makes holy' sinners within her ranks to the glory of God. It was to this end that Paul spoke when he said: 'Christ loved the

Church and gave himself up for her, that he might sanctify her, having cleansed her by the washing of water with the word, that he might present the Church to himself in splendor, without spot or wrinkle or any such thing, that she might be holy and without blemish (Eph 5:25-27). The bishop, as the chief steward of the Church of God and the symbol of holiness, guides the church in orthodoxy that translates to ethical behavior. Orthodoxy will lead to orthopathy. Orthopathy will lead to orthopraxis. Orthopraxis will ultimately lead to orthomartyrs.

The church is catholic in the sense that Jesus is the savior of all. Now this is a slippery slope in the days in which we live. Injurious doctrines of universal salvation and ultimate reconciliation are being heralded as the nullification of the righteous standard of God for holy living and submission to His will. Those who preach these heresies have hijacked the message of the cross and have added their uninitiated superimpositions in order to justify and support the receipt of salvation without the requisite of salvation. They have not understood the indicatives and imperatives of the mandates of sacred Scripture. There are those who take the truth of Christ's redemptive work and exploit it for their own profligate or divisive and seditions purposes. This expression of catholicity may be better articulated: Jesus is the savior of all those who would be saved.

The essence of the catholicity of the church may be couched and articulated in these words. The church is for all people at all times, called to take the gospel of Jesus Christ to every part of the world. The text of Scripture teaches: 'For God so love the world that He gave His only begotten son...' The nature of the gospel is that it is for everyone in every nation of every kindred from every tribe and in every tongue. This now begs the question of ecumenism or denominationalism, and requires of us an understood and accepted way of being in the world as a fellowship.

Finally, the church is apostolic. Christ established the church upon the foundation of the apostles and the prophets. It was founded upon the apostles in the sense that the apostolic memory was the guiding principle of the church. Christ commissioned the apostles to carry out his work into the various regions of the world to which they were sent. It was established upon the prophets in the sense that the church was the fulfillment of the prophetic declaration that God would draw out for Himself a people of every race, kindred, tribe and tongue. It is unquestionable that Christ chose and used the twelve not only to begin the church but also to carry out the work that He began through the church.

The assertion and acceptance of the apostolicity of the church begs the questions of the legitimacy of the leaders within the church. I mean this in two ways. In order to understand the apostolicity of the church one has to answer the question of whether a church itself can be adopted or co-opted into the body of Christ. Those Christian communities who had begun and were in full operation apart from the recorded influence of the church in Jerusalem had to reconcile this tension in the record of Scripture. The second question is: What is the importance or significance or even necessity of apostolic succession of bishops within the church? Are the bishops the legitimate successors to the apostles? These two questions have profound impact upon how we establish doctrine for the church and how we give expression governmentally and functionally.

Questions and Critiques

These and many other concerns are on the table for our thoughtful consideration. They have to do with competing questions of church government. The questions and critiques over apostles and bishops that have arisen particularly over the last three decades have often caused schisms and factions within Pentecostalism. These questions have principally centered on the ministry of the apostle and the office of the bishop. They have summoned our scholarly attention to discuss and to discover what dialogue exists between Scripture, history, tradition, and experience. Because the scope of these questions is vast, I will address only in the broadest terms, the prevailing questions that are being asked.

Is the apostle a gift or an office for the church today?

My reading of Scripture and understanding of history couches the ministry of the apostle squarely within the realm of a gift or grace upon the life of a Christian in order to carry out the ministry of Christ, functionally. Though some are calling it an 'office,' it was never alluded to in Scripture or understood in history to be an 'office.' I have argued that the apostles (who saw and walked with the Lord) were principally first century servants of Christ who heralded the story of Christ and carried the message of the gospel around the world. I have also argued that the bishops are the successors to the apostles. We are apostles who have been given an office by the church in which to function and direct the affairs of the church of the Lord Jesus Christ. Apostles exist today in the persons and office of bishops as ministry grace, not as an office in and of itself.

Didn't bishops corrupt the church throughout church history?

There are those who would argue for the apostle as an office and titular designation who would base their argument upon a supposed corruption of the entire church by the bishops. Though there was pollution within the ranks of the bishops as the result of human participation in the church, advocates for the apostolate seem to forget one of the apostles who was hand selected by Christ Himself corrupted the apostles of the Lamb through greed and conspiracy against our Lord. This argument typically frames the discussion for apostolate advocates. Those who make this claim fail to factor in all of the good, moral, faithful bishops of the Lord's church down through the centuries that looked to God in hope and shepherded the flock of God. There were many more good bishops than bad ones. Therefore, that argument holds very little merit for me.

We need apostles today because there was no spiritual criterion or qualifications for the bishopric in Scripture.

While it is true that the criterion delineated in Timothy and Titus bends toward the administrative, the moral, and the ethical. That does not imply that 'spiritual' criterion does not exist. A careful examination of sacred Scripture will reveal that the 'spiritual' criterion for apostles is nowhere in Scripture mandated. It has been my experience that many of those who espouse the apostolate as an office for the contemporary church, tend to invent criterion for the apostolic 'office' without Scripture or church history to support their claims. Some have even concocted apostolic levels and adjectives to describe their apostolate that are nowhere to be found in sacred Scripture. Though the criterion and imperative for bishops is moral, ethical, and administrative, the 'spiritual' criterion for the office of the bishop was understood, recognized, and affirmed by virtue of whom was receiving the charge contained in the epistle. Paul, who issued the edict, was writing to his sons Timothy and

Titus. Thus, he knew their spiritual estate and affirmed their spiritual maturity by reason of the appointment.

The church needs apostles today in order to further remove 'man-made' traditions from within her ranks.

While this statement sounds spiritual and maybe even sensible, a careful examination of its sub-stratum will reveal flaws in the logic of its implications. You see, this statement implies that man has no business collaborating with Christ in the building of the church. This is a false assertion and worthy of critique. Though Christ announced that He would build His church upon the rock, He has chosen to build it through and in cooperation with human agents. The synergy that Christ calls for in the building of the church requires the cooperation of the people (for our purposes the apostles and bishops) whom He assigned to work with Him.

Humans were given creative ability as a part of our created essence. Apostles and bishops have been called to use those creative abilities to worship Christ, fashion the church, and lift the spirituality of all believers. The supposed reconstitution of apostles for the purposes of removing 'man-made' traditions implies that they have some special and spiritual endowments not revealed to the entire body of Christ. I am more concerned about' apostles' with private revelation or personal instructions from Christ than I am with so-called 'man-made' traditions in the church given by bishops selected through biblical criterion.

Government and leadership in the African-American, Pentecostal tradition is an amalgamation of many aspects of liturgical, theological, historical, and cultural elements. There is no one correct form or style. The uniqueness of the localized government is often fleshed out in light of the people who make up the worshipping community. The beauty of the body is its diversity woven together with the unifying factors that typify the church. Apostles and bishops have been and continue to be the ministry and office that frame and lead the church into her future in God.

Bibliography

Alvarado, Johnathan E. "Twenty-First Century Holiness: Living at the Intersection of Wesleyan Theology & Contemporary Pentecostal Values" in Lee Roy Martin, ed., *A Future for Holiness: Pentecostal Explorations*. (Cleveland, TN: CPT Press, 2013).

Apostolic Commission, The. *Apostolic Biblical Statement and Practical Guidelines* (IPHC, Apostolic Commission, 2007).

Archbishop of Canterbury, The. "Address to the Third Global South to South Encounter" Red Sea, Egypt, October 25, 2005.

Archer, Kenneth J. *A Pentecostal Hermeneutic for the Twenty-first Century: Scripture, Spirit and Community*. New York: T & T Clark, International, 2004.

Arrington, French L. *The Acts of the Apostles: Introduction, Translation, and Commentary* (Cleveland, TN: Pathway Press, 1998).

Bakke, Ray. *A Theology As Big As the City*, (Downers Grove, IL: Intervarsity Press, 1997).

Biguzzi, Giancarlo "Witnessing Two by Two in the Acts of the Apostles" in *Biblica*, January 1, 2011.

Bond, Steve. "Apostle" in Chad Brand, Charles Draper, and Archie England (eds.) *The Holman Illustrated Bible Dictionary*. (Nashville, TN: Holman Bible Publishers, 2603).

Bruce, F. F. *New International Commentary on the New Testament Acts.* (Grand Rapids, MI: William B. Eerdman's Publishing Company, 1988).

Burkhard, John J. *Apostolicity Then and Now: An Ecumenical Church in a Postmodern World* (Collegeville, MN: Liturgical Press, 2004).

Carver, Robert Duncan. "Apostles and the Apostolate in the New Testament" in *Bibliotheca Sacra*, April-June 1977.

Clemmons, Ithiel. *Bishop C. H. Mason and the Church of God in Christ.* Lanham, MD: Pneuma Life Publications, 1996.

Cole, R. Alan. *Mark*, The New Testament Commentary (Grand Rapids, MI: InterVarsity Press, 1989).

Davids, Peter H. *The First Epistle to Peter*, New International Commentary on the New Testament (Grand Rapids, MI: William B. Eerdmans Publishing Company, 1990).

Dawn, Marva J. *Reaching Out without Dumbing Down: A Theology of Worship for This Urgent Time.* (Grand Rapids, MI: William B. Eerdmans Publishing Company, 1995)

Dayton, Donald. *Theological Roots of Pentecostalism* (Waco, TX: Baker Academic, 1987).

Dennis, Ralph L. *Divine Distinction: The Ministry of the Apostle, The Office of the Bishop.* (Baltimore, MD: Xulon Press.

"Didache, Xl: in Henry Bettenson & Chris Maunder (eds.), *Documents of the Christian Church* (Oxford, England: Oxford University Press, 2011).

Drury, Keith. *The Wonder of Worship: Why We Worship the Way We Do*. (Indianapolis, IN: Wesleyan Publishing House, 2005).

Eckhardt, John. *Moving in the Apostolic: God's Plan to Lead the Church to the Final Victory*. (Grand Rapids, MI: Chosen Books, 1999).

Englebrecht, Edward A. *The Church from Age to Age: A History from Galilee to Global Christianity*. (St. Louis, MO: Concordia Publishing, 2011).

Fee, Gordon. *1 and 2 Timothy, Titus, New* International Biblical Commentary, (Peabody, MA: Hendrickson Publishers, Inc., 1984).

_____. *The First Epistle to the Corinthians*, New International Biblical Commentary, (Peabody, MA: Hendrickson Publishers, Inc., 1984).

Fragments of Papias, 1.3-6, in ANF, 1: 153.

Gause, R. Hollis. *Revelation: God's Stamp of Sovereignty on History* (Cleveland, TN: Pathway Press, 1998).

Gonzalez, Justo L. *The History of Christian Thought Volume I: From the Beginnings to the Council of Chalcedon*. Nashville: Abingdon Press, 1970.

_____ *The Story of Christianity: Volume 1 The Early Church to the Dawn of the Reformation* (New York: Harper Collins Publishers, 1984).

Grudem, Wayne. *I Peter*, The Tyndale New Testament Commentary, (Grand Rapids, MI: William B. Eerdmans Publishing Company, 1988).

Guelich, Robert A. *Mark* World Bible Commentary (Dallas, TX: Word Books, 1989).

Guthrie, Donald. *Tyndale New Testament Commentaries: Pastoral Epistles*. (Grand Rapids, MI: William B. Eerdman's Nelson Publishing. 2000).

Hamon, Bill. *Apostles Prophets and the Coming Moves of God*, (Shippensburg, PA: Destiny Images, 1997).

Hillyer, Norman. *I and 2 Peter*, New International Bible Commentary, (Peabody, MA: Hendrickson Publishers, 1992).

Horton, Stanley M. and Gary B. McGee. *Systematic Theology: A Pentecostal Perspective*. Springfield, MO: Legion Books, 1994.

Hurtado, Larry W. *Mark*. New International Bible Commentary (Peabody, MA: Hendrickson Publishers, 1989).

Irvin, Dale T. and Scott W. Sunquist, *History of the World Christian Movement Volume I: Earliest Christianity to 1453*. (Maryknoll, New York: Orbis Books, 2009).

Kee, Doyle. "Who Were the 'Super-Apostles' of 2 Corinthians 10-13" in *Restoration Quarterly,* January 1, 1980.

Land, Steven J. "The Triune Center: Wesleyans and Pentecostals Together in Mission," in *Pneuma: The Journal of the Society for Pentecostal Studies*, Volume 21, Number, 2, Fall 1999).

Lane, William L. *Mark*, New International Commentary on the New Testament (Grand Rapids, MI: William B. Eerdman's Publishing Company, 1974).

Lockyer, Herbert. *All the Apostles of the Bible* (Grand Rapids, MI: Zondervan Publishing House, 1972).

Marshall, Howard. *New International Commentary on the New Testament Luke* (Grand Rapids, MI: William B. Eerdman's Publishing Company, 1980).

Morris, Leon. *1 Corinthians*, The New Testament Commentary (Grand Rapids, MI: William B. Eerdman's Publishing. 1985).

_____*Revelation*, The New Testament Commentary (Grand Rapids, MI: William B. Eerdman's Publishing Company, 1987)'

Mounce, Robert H. *The Book of Revelation*, New International Commentary on the New Testament (Grand Rapids, MI: William B. Eerdman's Publishing Company, 1998).

Mounce, William. The World Biblical Commentary: Pastoral Epistles, (Nashville, TN: Thomas Nelson Publishers, Inc. 2000).

Olson, Roger J. *The Story of Christianity Theology*. Downers Grove, IL: InterVarsity Press. 1999.

Saucy, Robert L. *The Church in God's Program*, (Chicago, IL; Moody Press, 1972).

Scaer, Peter. "Luke and the Foundations of the Church," in *Concordia Theological Quarterly* 76 (2012).

Shelley, Bruce L. *Church History in Plain Language*. (Dallas, TX: Word Publishing, 1995).

Soards, Marion L. *1 Corinthians*, New International Bible Commentary (Peabody, MA: Hendrickson Publishers, 1999).

Sullivan, Francis A. *From Apostles to Bishops; The Development of the Episcopacy in the Early Church* (New York: The Newman Press, 2001).

Vines, Jerry. *Exploring the Gospels: Mark* (Neptune, NJ: Loizeaux Brothers, 1990).

Wagner, C. Peter *Apostles and Prophets: The Foundations of the Church*. (Ventura CA: Regal Books, 2000).

Walls, A. F. "Apostle" in L. Howard Marshall, A. R. Millard, J. I. Packer, and D. J. Wiseman (eds.) *New Bible Dictionary* (Downers Grove, IL: IVP Academic, 1996).

Wall, Robert W. *Revelation*, New International Bible Commentary (Peabody, MA: Hendrickson Publishers, 1991).

Williams, David J. *Acts*, New International Bible Commentary (Peabody, MA: Hendrickson Publishers, 1990).

ABOUT THE AUTHOR

Bishop Johnathan Elliott Alvarado

Johnathan E. Alvarado, DMin is a family man, the Pastor of Grace Church International, the Bishop of the Grace Fellowship of Churches International, a Pentecostal theologian, and an educator. He began in ministry as a twelve-year-old preacher at Union Grove Baptist Church in Columbus, Ohio, under the late Dr. Phale D. Hale. He earned a Bachelor of Arts degree in Music from Morehouse College in 1990 where he performed with the world-renowned Morehouse College Glee Club, serving as accompanist and Student Director under the baton of the late Dr. Wendell P. Whalum.

Bishop Alvarado has served as Minister of Music at churches throughout Atlanta in the late 1980s and early 1990's. His love for education and music led him to begin his teaching career as an elementary school music teacher in the DeKalb County School System for five years, then, as a seminary professor. He also served as Music Director for gospel music artist Daryl Coley from 1985-94.

In 1991 Bishop Alvarado began holding Friday night Bible studies and by June of 1992 with three adults and nine teenagers, he was ordained pastor/teacher and commissioned to establish Total Grace Christian Center (now Grace Church International) by his father in the faith, Apostle LaFayette Scales. Under Bishop Alvarado's leadership, Grace Church International has grown to nearly 3000 members and over 25 active ministries in DeKalb and Clayton County, Georgia. The church is celebrated for its intimate praise and worship, passionate preaching, commitment to wholesome family, educational emphasis, and ministry to the community.

In 2005, Alvarado was elected Presiding Bishop of the Grace Fellowship of Churches International and was consecrated to this sacred office in June, 2006. He is a member of the Joint College of African America Pentecostal Bishops where he serves as the Chair of the Advisory Board and Academic Dean.

Bishop Alvarado has earned a Master of Arts in Ministry at Luther Rice Seminary in Lithonia, Georgia, a Master of Divinity Degree from the Church of God Theological Seminary, in Cleveland, Tennessee, a Doctor of Ministry Degree in Leadership and Renewal from Regent University School of Divinity in Virginia Beach, Virginia, and a Master of Theology Degree from Columbia Theological Seminary, Decatur, Georgia. His awards and honors include election into the Morehouse College Board of Preachers, the prestigious F.J. May Preaching Award, The Divinity Outstanding Doctoral Student Award and many civic, community and state commendations. Additionally, he is honored to serve as a Chaplain and Leadership Consultant to the DeKalb County Sheriff's Office.

As a seminary professor, Bishop Alvarado has taught and guest lectured at colleges, seminaries, and universities, such as Beulah Heights University (Atlanta, GA), Howard University School of Divinity (Washington, DC), McAfee School of Theology, Mercer University (Atlanta, GA), Columbia International University Seminary and School of World Missions (Columbia, SC), Regent University School of Divinity (Virginia Beach, VA), Pentecostal Theological Seminary (Cleveland, TN), Georgia Piedmont Technical College (Clarkston, GA), and Southeastern University (Lakeland, FL). Currently, he serves as President of Theology at the Greater Atlanta Theological Seminary. He is also a member of the American Academy of Religion and the Society for Pentecostal Studies. As an scholar, Alvarado has authored academic papers, essays, and journal articles on Ecclesiology, Church/Pastoral Leadership, Holiness, Worship and Liturgics that are being used in classrooms, seminars and workshops throughout the country.

Bishop and Dr. Toni G. Alvarado, his co-pastor and wife of twenty-eight years, are the proprietors of Targeted Living, LLC a coaching, consulting, and publishing company. Together, they co-authored, Let's Stay Together: Relationship Strategies For Successful Marriages, co-pastor They are the proud parents of Johnathan Elliott II (22), Joshua Elisha (21), and Ariel Antoinette (19). He and his wife serve as role models to countless families on how to strike the delicate balance of a healthy life at home, work, and church.

www.ingramcontent.com/pod-product-compliance
Lightning Source LLC
Chambersburg PA
CBHW070108080526
44586CB00013B/1231